Clay Ham

Foundations of Contemporary Interpretation

Moisés Silva, Series Editor

Volume 1

HAS CHUR MISREAD THE BIBLE?

D0885127

THE HISTORY OF INTERPRETATION IN THE LIGHT OF CURRENT ISSUES

Moisés Silva

Academie
Books Grand Rapids, Michigan
Zondervan Publishing House

HAS THE CHURCH MISREAD THE BIBLE?

Copyright © 1987 by
Moisés Silva

ACADEMIE BOOKS is an imprint of Zondervan Publishing House
1415 Lake Drive, S.E.
Grand Rapids, Michigan 49506

Library of Congress Cataloging in Publication Data

Silva, Moises
      Has the church misread the Bible?

      (Foundations of contemporary interpretation ; v. 1)
      Bibliography: p.
      Includes indexes.
            1. Bible—Hermeneutics.   2. Bible—Criticism,
interpretation, etc.—History.   I. Title.   II. Series.
BS476.S55   1987   220.6'01   87–14476
ISBN   0–310–40921–7

Edited by Craig Noll
Designed by Louise Bauer

Printed in the United States of America

89   90   91   92 / EP / 10   9   8   7   6   5   4   3   2

Dedicated to the Memory of My Revered Teacher

EDWARD J. YOUNG

erudite scholar and humble believer,
whose hermeneutics reflected no conflict
between devotion to the Scriptures
and regard for the intellect

CONTENTS

PREFACE

The first chapter of this book serves as an introduction to the series *Foundations of Contemporary Interpretation* as a whole. It is therefore unnecessary here to describe its purpose in detail.

It may be useful, however, to point out that all of the contributors, committed as they are to the divine authority of Scripture, assume from the start that a right relationship with its divine author is the most fundamental prerequisite for proper biblical interpretation. The point needs to be stressed here precisely because the series itself does not attempt to develop that truth. This volume and those that follow it are addressed primarily to readers who share such a commitment with the authors.

The problem is that this theological conviction, while essential for a true understanding of Scripture, does not by itself guarantee that we will interpret Scripture aright. We have become increasingly aware that the interpretation of *any* document is fraught with many and serious difficulties. What, then, are those principles that concern *general* hermeneutics? And how do those principles bear on our understanding of the Bible?

A satisfactory response to these questions requires the concerted effort of scholars who are willing to move beyond the narrow confines of exegesis as such. Indeed, one is hard-pressed to think of an academic discipline that does not have something substantive to contribute to our concerns. Each volume in the present series addresses one discipline that seems distinctly promising in aiding the work of biblical exegesis.

Our main audience consists of seminary students who have at least an initial acquaintance with theological scholarship and who are willing to ask the hard questions, even when simple answers are nowhere to be found. As seminarians prepare to take positions of leadership in ecclesiastical and academic settings, this important period in their theological formation must develop in them a genuine appreciation of the foundational problems faced by biblical exegetes. Perhaps our efforts will aid today's students to provide some of the answers we ourselves have failed to give them.

The series is intended, however, to reach a broader readership as well. On the one hand, each contributor will seek to make the material clear and accessible to lay Christians who see the need to be fully informed in this important field of hermeneutics. On the other hand, the volumes will be carefully documented in the footnotes so that advanced students and scholars can pursue special points of interest in the literature.

The reader should note that the term *hermeneutics* is used here in its traditional sense, namely, the study of those principles that should guide our work of interpretation. This decision, however, is not meant to prejudge the question whether biblical hermeneutics should concern itself with the present significance of a text (and not only with its original meaning). On the contrary, this issue will occupy us repeatedly in the course of the series.

The more recent term *hermeneutic,* though often used to describe a specific approach to interpretation (as in "the new hermeneutic"), is rather vague. We shall avoid this term except in certain contexts in which a contrast with *hermeneutics* is necessary. Unless otherwise specified, no distinction is intended between the terms *presupposition* and *preunderstanding*—much less by the use of such pairs of words as *interpretive/interpretative* (the first of which, though sometimes ridiculed, has a noble pedigree reaching back to at least the eighteenth century), *method/methodology, synonymy/synonymity,* etc. On stylistic questions of this sort, the authors will follow their own preferences.

The present series is launched with the conviction, not only that the Christian church faces a grave challenge, but also that God, who has not left his people alone, will surely guide them to a full knowledge of his truth.

ABBREVIATIONS

AARTT	American Academy of Religion Texts and Translations
AnBib	Analecta biblica
ANF	*The Ante-Nicene Fathers*
ANRW	*Anstieg und Niedergang der römischen Welt*
BGBH	Beitrag zur Geschichte der biblischen Hermeneutik
BSac	*Bibliotheca sacra*
CHB	*The Cambridge History of the Bible*
GNT	Grundrisse zum Neuen Testament
HAC	*Hermeneutics, Authority, and Canon*
HIB	*Hermeneutics, Inerrancy, and the Bible*
ICBI	International Council for Biblical Inerrancy
IDB	*The Interpreter's Dictionary of the Bible*
Int	*Interpretation*
ISBE	*The International Standard Bible Encyclopedia* (rev. ed.)
JHI	*Journal of the History of Ideas*
JSOT	*Journal for the Study of the Old Testament*
MSU	Mitteilungen der Septuaginta-Unternehmens
NPNF	*The Nicene and Post-Nicene Fathers*
PTS	Patristische Texte und Studien
RGG	*Die Religion in Geschichte und Gegenwart*
SBLMS	Society of Biblical Literature Monograph Series
SBS	Stuttgarter Bibelstudien
SJT	*Scottish Journal of Theology*
WTJ	*Westminster Theological Journal*

1

TODAY'S HERMENEUTICAL CHALLENGE

The radio speaker that Sunday morning was a successful minister in one of the major Protestant denominations. His text was Acts 5. His topic was "power." He spoke eloquently of the many ways in which most of us misuse our authority. Parents abuse their children by their negativism. Government leaders show insensitivity to the pains of those in need. We destroy by our criticism when we should build up with our praise.

As he approached the last part of his radio message, the preacher finally came to his text. In the narrative of Acts he found a dramatic example of the misuse of power. Ananias and Sapphira, weak Christians who had just given in to their temptations, were in need of reassurance and upbuilding. The apostle Peter, in an ugly display of arrogance, abused his authority and denounced their conduct with awful threats. Terror consumed each of them in turn, and they died on the spot under Peter's unbearable invective.

Most readers of this book will no doubt shake their heads in unbelief at such an example of biblical interpretation. But how can we account for it? This preacher was not an ignoramus but a very well-educated minister serving a sophisticated middle-class parish in a Philadelphia suburb. The exegetical tools he was given during his theological training were probably not significantly different from those of most other

1

seminarians. Most disturbing of all, the very *process* going on in his mind as he arrived at an interpretation of Acts 5 was basically the same process all of us use—not only in interpreting Scripture but also in our understanding of a social conversation, the morning paper, or the evening news.

The history of the Christian church, like the history of society generally, has been characterized by repeated conflicts regarding the interpretation of evidence. Precisely because Christians place enormous significance on the Bible, disagreements regarding *biblical* evidence can have serious consequences.

In our day, however, "the hermeneutical issue" has surfaced with a vengeance. Only a generation ago, conservative Christians enjoyed a sense of unity in their interpretation of the Bible. They knew, of course, that differences existed among various denominations and that some of these differences touched on matters of considerable importance, such as the meaning and practice of baptism, the proper understanding of sanctification, expectations regarding the end times, and so on. Relatively few people, however, seemed to appreciate the implications of this state of affairs; and no one was arguing that Evangelicals were faced with a hermeneutical crisis.

There must be some way to account for that period of innocence. Perhaps it is simply that a conservative Methodist could listen to a conservative Baptist and agree with 99 percent of what he or she heard. A sermon on the parable of the Prodigal Son would sound basically the same, whether it came from a Pentecostal evangelist or from a Presbyterian theologian. With so much obvious agreement, who would stop to worry about differences in interpretation?

But things have changed. As many have pointed out, one can no longer assume that an individual who professes an evangelical faith will hold "the party line" on key social and ethical issues such as capital punishment, abortion, nuclear armament, divorce, premarital sex, or homosexuality.

> Contemporary evangelicals are finding it difficult to achieve anything like a consensus on each succeeding theological topic they address. Moreover, they seem stymied in any effort toward

unity, unable to agree on a collective interpretive strategy for moving beyond their current impasse. . . . If evangelicals cannot discover a way to move more effectively toward theological consensus, can they still maintain in good conscience their claim to Biblical authority as a hallmark?[1]

Gone are the days when one could predict where a biblical scholar would come down on the date of the Exodus, the authorship of Isaiah, and comparable critical questions. As if to dramatize the depth of the hermeneutical disarray, conservatives could not even agree on how to handle the publication, in 1982, of a commentary by a prominent evangelical scholar who argued that many events related in the Gospel of Matthew are not to be interpreted as fully historical.[2]

Already in the late 1970s, members of the International Council for Biblical Inerrancy recognized the need to address hermeneutical principles if their claims for biblical authority were to mean anything and, as a result, held the ICBI Summit II in 1982. Sixteen papers, covering a wide range of topics in the area of hermeneutics, were presented and discussed at this meeting and then published in a hefty volume.[3] The participants represented the conservative wing of Evangelicalism and thus from the start agreed on some very basic issues. Moreover, they reached the necessary consensus to produce a significant document, "The Chicago Statement on Biblical Hermeneutics."

And yet all was not well. A reviewer of *HIB* commented,

I was left with a nagging question: if, as the participants affirm, the meaning in each biblical text is "single, definite and fixed"

---

[1] Robert K. Johnston, *Evangelicals at an Impasse: Biblical Authority in Practice* (Atlanta: John Knox, 1979), pp. 147 and 7.

[2] Robert H. Gundry, *Matthew: A Commentary on His Literary and Theological Art* (Grand Rapids: Eerdmans, 1982). For a summary of the controversy, which led to Gundry's resignation from the Evangelical Theological Society, see *Christianity Today* 28:2 (Feb. 3, 1984): 36–38.

[3] Earl D. Radmacher and Robert D. Preus, eds., *Hermeneutics, Inerrancy, and the Bible* (Grand Rapids: Zondervan, 1984), hereafter *HIB*. Note, incidentally, Elliott Johnson's comment: "In a sense, evangelicals have lived with an interpretational truce" (p. 409).

and applies to all cultural contexts, and the Holy Spirit alone enables believers to apply the scripture to their lives, to what purpose are these nine hundred pages of argument?[4]

Although this objection reveals a failure to grasp the intent of the participants, the Chicago Statement nevertheless makes biblical interpretation sound easier than it often is. The very discussions at the summit show that the participants, when dealing with a number of crucial interpretive issues, found oneness of mind to be a very distant hope indeed.[5]

One attempt to deal with this hermeneutical crisis has been to argue that the doctrine of inerrancy *entails* certain interpretive positions. In the face of turmoil, this approach is very tempting because it appears to eliminate, with one stroke, a variety of undesirable viewpoints.

Such a move, however, has desperation written all over it, and it undermines the very task of interpretation. The truth of scriptural authority does not automatically tell us what a given passage means: it does assure us that, once we have correctly identified the biblical teaching (in other words, proper interpretation is assumed), that teaching may be trusted unequivocally.[6] At any rate, the very events that have led to the present crisis show rather clearly—unpleasant as this may sound—that a sincere and intelligent commitment to the classical doctrine of biblical inerrancy in no way guarantees that an individual will adopt expected interpretations.

One could argue that the present impasse is the result of accumulated hermeneutical assumptions, unspoken and even

---

[4] C. S. Rodd, *Book List* (n.p.: Society for Old Testament Study, 1986), p. 94.

[5] See esp. chaps. 2, 4, and 7, dealing respectively with historical problems, normativeness, and authorial intention. Other evangelical scholars, though themselves clearly committed to inerrancy, from time to time express dissatisfaction with some aspects of ICBI; see D. A. Carson and John D. Woodbridge, eds., *Hermeneutics, Authority, and Canon* (Grand Rapids: Zondervan, 1986), hereafter *HAC*, pp. 7, 64–69. As the following material will make clear, however, the current "hermeneutical crisis" affects others besides Evangelicals. Fundamental interpretive questions are being debated across the various fields of biblical scholarship, conservative and liberal alike.

[6] I have treated this matter in greater detail in my inaugural lecture, "Old Princeton, Westminster, and Inerrancy," forthcoming in *WTJ* 50 (1988).

unconscious. And it is probably no accident that similar tensions have surfaced in other fields, including literary criticism and science. *Foundations of Contemporary Interpretation* is an attempt to make a positive contribution to this general problem by drawing on a variety of disciplines. We hope thereby to focus on the debate at its most fundamental level. This level is not that of "special hermeneutics" (the specific principles one must keep in mind when interpreting prophecy, parables, etc.), nor is it a question of determining whether a particular critical tool (form criticism, redaction criticism, etc.) is legitimate. Rather we are concerned with the basic processes that affect our understanding of everything we see, hear, or read.

Scholars have traditionally used the term *general hermeneutics* to identify our topic, and the most successful writers in this field have cast their net widely in their attempt to identify those elements that characterize the sane interpretation of any document.[7] This task has been made more difficult by the explosion of knowledge in the twentieth century. The present series seeks to introduce the student to those areas that seem to provide the most relevant points of contact with biblical interpretation. I survey here six of these areas.

PHILOSOPHY

One of the most remarkable developments in the history of philosophy took place at the beginning of this century, when a number of leading British thinkers, disenchanted with much of current philosophical reflection, concluded that the real business of philosophy was not to build speculative systems but simply to analyze the way language is used. This apparently modest goal led to an almost complete reorientation of the way "one does philosophy" in Britain and America. *Analytical Philosophy,* whatever its weaknesses, has had some salutary

---

[7] See the old classic by Milton S. Terry, *Biblical Interpretation: A Treatise on the Interpretation of the Old and New Testaments,* rev. ed. (New York: Easton & Maines, 1890), p. 17. Friedrich Schleiermacher is usually regarded as the first scholar to insist that biblical hermeneutics must be part of a general theory of understanding.

effects, especially through its emphasis on the study of linguistic data.[8]

Across the English Channel, to be sure, it was pretty much business as usual. And yet even in the Continent, philosophers were showing increasing interest in the phenomenon of language. In their case, it was a matter of pursuing questions that have plagued philosophers even before Socrates decided to make a nuisance of himself. More to the point, some nineteenth-century idealists had expended considerable effort seeking to develop an encompassing (and speculative) philosophy of language. This interest forms part of the background for the development of certain movements, particularly existentialism, that have had great impact on the course taken by European philosophers in the twentieth century.[9]

This idealist tradition is vulnerable to some powerful criticisms, yet within the context of that tradition some of the most crucial questions about hermeneutics have arisen. Such thinkers as Martin Heidegger, for example, have forced us to take seriously the role that *preunderstanding* plays in the process of interpretation.[10] None of us is able to approach new data with a blank mind, and so our attempts to understand new information consist largely of adjusting our prior "framework of understanding"—integrating the new into the old.

These ideas have immediate consequences for the way we interpret the Bible and do theology. The common insistence that we should approach the text without any prior ideas

---

[8] Particularly striking is the way modern linguists, though starting from quite different perspectives and interested in "purely scientific" endeavors, have developed formulations that coincide significantly with those of Anglo-Saxon philosophers. See M. Silva, *Biblical Words and Their Meaning: An Introduction to Lexical Semantics* (Grand Rapids: Zondervan, 1983), p. 106n.

[9] For a brief but useful description of Continental views on language, see Kenneth Hamilton, *Words and the Word* (Grand Rapids: Eerdmans, 1971), pp. 28–36.

[10] The views of Heidegger are treated, among other works, in Richard E. Palmer, *Hermeneutics: Interpretation Theory in Schleiermacher, Dilthey, Heidegger, and Gadamer* (Evanston: Northwestern University Press, 1969), and in Anthony C. Thiselton, *The Two Horizons: New Testament Hermeneutics and Philosophical Description* (Grand Rapids: Eerdmans, 1980).

regarding its meaning becomes almost irrelevant. And the standard advice given to theological students to study the text before consulting commentaries, or to determine its meaning before considering its application, appears self-defeating. Perhaps we are unable to find out what a passage meant to its original audience except by way of our own situation!

Could it be that it is impossible to shed our presuppositions precisely because it is they that mediate understanding? If so, do we drown in our subjectivity and abandon the goal of objective exegesis? Is every interpretive effort destined to be relativized by the reality of our situation?

One can hardly think of a more fundamental set of questions to ask. These questions will not go away, and adequate answers require careful and patient reflection. One of the volumes in this series will seek to clarify the nature of the problem and suggest responsible approaches toward a solution.

LITERARY CRITICISM

Philosophical discussions about meaning are quickly taken up by literary critics—understandably so, since their livelihood depends on their ability to say something about what a literary piece "means." In their own way, however, critics have contributed significantly to the present skepticism.

A few generations ago, it seemed obvious to all that a student of literature was supposed to determine the intention of the original author of a piece. Great effort was therefore expended on discovering as much as possible about the author, the circumstances in which the piece was written, and so forth. But then a reaction developed among a number of scholars who argued that the literary piece itself had an existence quite independent of its author. The meaning of the composition, therefore, could not be tied to the author's intention. New questions were being posed, particularly with regard to the ambiguity that is so characteristic of poetry.

Instead of asking "Does the text mean this or that?" with a "Tea or coffee?" intonation, implying that only one answer can be chosen, critics began to ask "Can the text mean this or that?" with a "Cigarettes or liquor?" intonation, seeing a text as a bag of mysteries not advertised on the surface. (There is some debate whether the author knows what he has packed.) To take an example, in Marvell's lines:

> Meanwhile the mind, from pleasure less,
> Withdraws into its happiness

should we understand that the mind is less because of pleasure or that because of pleasure the mind withdraws? The answer now was to be "Both—and what else can you find?"[11]

When some of the philosophical currents discussed previously join forces with this approach to literature, the results can be unnerving. Some years back E. D. Hirsch mounted a valiant attack on these forces by presenting a fresh argument that supported the importance of an author's intent. He has truly been a voice crying in the wilderness, however, and the current scholarly orthodoxy views him as something of an anomaly. He, has found, to be sure, a very receptive audience among evangelical theologians, although enthusiasm for his argument seems to be declining.[12]

At any rate, it is worthwhile noting here that the classic formulations of the doctrine of inerrancy placed considerable emphasis on the need to ascertain the intention, or purpose, of the biblical author. Surely one cannot attribute infallibility to arbitrary and haphazard inferences from a biblical passage—one must know what the writer "really meant." In one of the

---

[11] G. W. Turner, *Stylistics* (Baltimore: Penguin, 1973), pp. 100–101. Turner further remarks, "If intention is not to be the criterion for understanding a poem, should a poet read reviews of his own poetry to find out what it means? If he disagrees with a consensus of critics, who is right?" (p. 148).

[12] E. D. Hirsch, Jr., *Validity in Interpretation* (New Haven: Yale University Press, 1967). Though critical of Hirsch in some important respects, Charles Altieri takes seriously and reformulates some elements of his work; see Altieri, *Act and Quality: A Theory of Literary Meaning and Humanistic Understanding* (Amherst: University of Massachusetts Press, 1981), chap. 3, esp. pp. 143–59. Hirsch is referred to frequently in *HIB*. On the other hand, note the qualifications expressed by Vern S. Poythress in "Analysing a Biblical Text: Some Important Linguistic Distinctions," *SJT* 32 (1979): 113–37.

fundamental papers expounding the evangelical view of inspiration, Hodge and Warfield assumed that the primary question to be asked was that of the biblical author's "professed or implied purpose." They asserted: "Exegesis must be historical as well as grammatical, and must always seek the meaning *intended,* not any meaning that can be tortured out of a passage."[13]

In view of this connection between the doctrine of infallibility and the need to determine the biblical writer's intended meaning, one can see that recent developments in literary criticism have clear implications for biblical authority. Some contemporary voices have in fact argued (rather naïvely, it seems to me) that Evangelicals ought to stop wasting their time fussing over inerrancy: after all, these critics claim, any appeal to an author's intent is passé!

But there is more. In recent years a growing number of biblical scholars have argued for the need to use the tools and methods of literary criticism in the interpretation of the Bible. A thriving section in the Society of Biblical Literature, for example, is devoted to rhetorical criticism, which attempts to understand biblical material as carefully composed literary works.

The extent to which the Bible may or may not be viewed as a work of art has long been a matter of debate, with no less a literary critic than C. S. Lewis arguing that, because of its sacred character, Scripture

> does not invite, it excludes or repels, the merely aesthetic approach. You can read it as literature only by a *tour de force*. You are cutting the wood against the grain, using the tool for a purpose it was not intended to serve. It demands incessantly to be taken on its own terms: it will not continue to give literary delight very long except to those who go for it for something quite different.[14]

---

[13] A. A. Hodge and B. B. Warfield, *Inspiration* (Grand Rapids: Baker, 1979; orig. 1881), pp. 42–43. On the problems associated with such terms as *purpose* and *intention,* see my article "Old Princeton, Westminster, and Inerrancy."

[14] C. S. Lewis, *The Literary Impact of the Authorised Version* (London: University of London, 1950), p. 25.

Any person's view on this question will depend largely on how the expression *work of art* is understood, but no reasonable person is likely to deny that, at least in some sense, the biblical books are literature and therefore patient of literary study. Again, different scholars will view specific approaches, such as that of structuralism, with varying degrees of sympathy, but all will recognize that literary sensitivity is a significant aid to the appreciation of the Bible.

The question becomes truly problematic, however, in the attempt to relate literature and history. Earlier biblical scholarship (both liberal and conservative) is often criticized for paying too much attention to the historicity of biblical stories. If conservative scholars wonder what may have motivated a biblical character to act in a particular way, they are chastised for focusing on the historical event rather than on the literary skills of the biblical author. If liberal scholars ridicule a conservative reading of some historical portion, they too are criticized for missing the point. In other words, we are told that asking historical kinds of questions is basically irrelevant. One proponent of this point of view suggests that "the new literary criticism may be described as inherently ahistorical." He further comments: "Consideration of the Bible as literature is itself the beginning and end of scholarly endeavor. The Bible is taken first and finally as a literary object."[15]

In view of this wide range of complicated and intimidating questions, one of the most demanding volumes in our series will be devoted to literary approaches in the interpretation of the Scriptures.

LINGUISTICS

Some years back, while visiting an evangelical seminary, I was having lunch with several students, and the conversation turned, as it so often does, to the question of whether learning the biblical languages is really necessary. One of the students,

---

[15] D. Robertson, "Literature, the Bible as," *IDB Supplementary Volume,* pp. 547–51, esp. p. 548.

who gave every indication of being highly motivated, raised the issue in a particularly interesting way. "I can appreciate," he said, "the value and importance of learning Greek. There are many passages in the New Testament in which the author's meaning becomes clearer by paying attention to the precise nuances and distinctions he's using. But I don't find that's the case with Hebrew. One spends a lot of time and effort on Hebrew but there seems to be very little pay-off."

No doubt many other students have felt the same way (to judge by the number of ministers that do not keep up their Hebrew). In one sense we may agree with this student's evaluation. Relative to the Old Testament, the New Testament contains much more material of an expressly theological character. Jesus' debates with his opponents, for example, and Paul's polemical writings often require a kind of attention to details that may be unnecessary, or even inappropriate, when studying Old Testament narrative or poetry.

To put it differently, much of the Old Testament consists of material written in a somewhat expansive style, in which repetition and stylistic variations play a prominent role; in such a case, meaning is conveyed by the impact of large sections as a whole and seldom by the precise force of individual words and sentences. In a passage such as Galatians 3, however, a great deal of conceptual richness is concentrated within brief sections; as a result, one is frequently faced by conflicting interpretations of individual clauses.

But the student to whom I was speaking did not really have in mind differences in content and style. The very fact that Hebrew is Hebrew, he seemed to think, makes it less susceptible to exegetical richness. My response to him was not that he had failed to appreciate the special nuances of Hebrew words and syntax; rather, I argued that he was probably misusing his Greek.

In the interest of encouraging students to learn their Greek well, many teachers and writers have unwittingly created an unrealistic picture of how language works. A large number of people, for example, perceive Greek as perhaps the richest and most precise language that has ever been used, and it is taken for granted that Greek writers must have exploited semantic nuances, subtle tense distinctions, and syntactic variations to express their meaning in the fullest and clearest fashion possible.

Part of the problem is that in the nineteenth century the leading philologists shared an exaggerated high opinion of the classical languages.[16] Since Greek culture and literature had undoubtedly reached levels of greatness, it was assumed that a similar greatness must be attributed to the linguistic medium, that is, to the very *form* of communication. Understandably, Christians deduced that God must have chosen Greek as the medium to communicate the gospel because it was the "best" language available. With regard to the New Testament too, therefore, there was a tendency to confuse the value of the message with that of the medium. The following quotation is only one of many typical assessments:

> The Greek language is the beautiful flower, the elegant jewel, the most finished masterpiece of Indo-Germanic thought. . . . Its syntax is organized on the most perfect system. . . . [With the coming of the gospel] the Greek language had now to perform a work for which it had providentially been preparing, and yet one which it had never yet attempted, namely, to convey the divine revelation to mankind. [As a result the language was] employed by the Spirit of God, and transformed and transfigured, yes, glorified, with a light and sacredness that the classic literature never possessed.[17]

In the early decades of this century, however, a radically new conception of language began to develop. One important contributing factor in this change was the discovery and careful

---

[16] According to Edward Sapir, most nineteenth-century "linguistic theorists themselves spoke languages of a certain type, of which the most fully developed varieties were the Latin and Greek that they had learned in their childhood. It was not difficult for them to be persuaded that these familiar languages represented the 'highest' development that speech had yet attained and that all other types were but steps on the way to this beloved 'inflective' type" (*Language: An Introduction to the Study of Speech* [New York: Harcourt, Brace & World, 1949; orig. 1921], p. 123).

[17] Charles A. Briggs, *General Introduction to the Study of Holy Scripture,* rev. ed. (Grand Rapids: Baker, 1970; orig. 1900), pp. 64, 67, 70–71.

study of numerous "primitive" languages that proved to be every bit as complicated as Greek. The system of five or more cases found in the classical languages cannot hold a candle, for example, to the numerous morphological distinctions that exist in the Bantu tongues. And if the verbal system of Greek seems involved, what is one to say of Basque?

Moreover, it is now clear that the number of vocabulary items—and the consequent potential for semantic distinctions—in a language is a function of the interests and needs of a particular society, not a quality inherent in the language itself. Certainly the lexicon of contemporary English exceeds by many times what was available in Ancient Greek. And in spite of frequent warnings that linguistic corruptions have set English on a course of self-destruction, it is arguable that the morphological and syntactic simplicity into which English has evolved has resulted in a more flexible, efficient, and enduring system of communication.[18]

Be that as it may, the modern study of language (general linguistics) affects quite directly the way we interpret ancient texts like the Bible. The value of studying the biblical languages does not reside in its potential for displaying exegetical razzle-dazzle. In fact, striking interpretations that lean too heavily, sometimes exclusively, on subtle grammatical distinctions are seldom worth considering. On the other hand, genuine familiarity with Greek (and Hebrew!) develops sensitivity and maturity in the interpreter and allows his or her decisions to be built on a much broader base of information. More often than not, the fruit of language learning is intangible: it remains in the background, providing the right perspective for responsible exegesis.

Linguistics, however, does more than alter our attitude to the study of the biblical languages. It formulates principles and provides techniques for the analysis of written and oral communication. One volume in this series will summarize

---

[18] See Otto Jespersen, *Language: Its Nature, Development, and Origin* (New York: Norton, 1964; orig. 1921), pp. 332–34.

those areas of modern linguistics that appear most relevant for the development of biblical hermeneutics.

HISTORY

Still another volume in this series will be devoted to a very important set of questions arising from the fact that the biblical books were written within the context of an ancient culture. As we noted in our discussion of literary criticism, some scholars would argue that concern over history has been detrimental to biblical interpretation—that asking the question "What really happened?" has distracted us from the more important issue, "What is the *text* really saying?"

There clearly is a measure of truth in that criticism. Many of us are tempted to speculate about historical questions that are not at all addressed by the text (e.g., where did Cain get his wife? did Paul know that the earth is not flat?), and so we fall into the danger of missing the thrust of the passage itself. As usually formulated, however, the criticism implies a facile dichotomy between history and literature, and most biblical scholars would insist that the historical approach must continue to hold some sort of priority in the interpretive task. We should not infer that all of these scholars have high regard for the trustworthiness of the biblical narratives. Unfortunately, a good many specialists have concluded that significant portions of the Bible have little or no factual basis. And while the mainstream of biblical scholarship does not show nearly the degree of skepticism that was common a couple of generations ago, *some* skepticism is regarded as essential to the historical method.[19] As

---

[19] Part of the reason for skepticism, of course, is that historians in all fields are expected to judge the reliability of their sources; see Marc Bloch, *The Historian's Craft* (New York: Knopf, 1963), chap. 3, "Historical Criticism," the most substantial chapter in the book, devoted to developing an informed skepticism. But biblical scholars, more often than not, find it necessary to make the point that the Bible cannot be trusted implicitly; see, for example, W. G. Kümmel, *The New Testament: The History of the Investigation of Its Problems* (Nashville: Abingdon, 1972), esp. p. 30, where the author, after praising the sixteenth-century Reformer M. Flacius, proceeds to condemn his approach as unhistorical on the grounds that Flacius did not allow for contradictions in Scripture.

a result, a growing number of conservative scholars are becoming hesitant to apply the doctrine of infallibility to all the historical claims of Scripture.

The hermeneutical implications are obvious. Does a narrative passage in the Old Testament *mean* what it appears to be saying? If it does, according to some scholars, one still needs to decide whether the story is *factual* or not, whether the biblical author was accurate or in error. The other approach—that of some literary critics—argues that the passage does *not* mean what it appears to be saying, that the historical question is more or less irrelevant for determining the meaning of the passage.

To further complicate this discussion, one must consider the character of ancient historiography. Quite apart from the "literature versus history" debate, it is clear that contemporary historians produce works that differ in some important respects from ancient historical sources. What with quotation marks, square brackets, ellipsis points, footnotes, and so on, modern readers expect a measure of precision that was unknown to the ancients.

But just how great are the differences between the two types of history writing? And to what extent do differences in literary genre affect our answer to this question? Most evangelical scholars recognize that the discourses in the Book of Job, whatever their historical basis, reflect a certain measure of literary creativity. Not many, however, are ready to concede that the Book of Jonah relates a fictional story. Fewer still would agree that the gospel writers embellished their narratives with made-up stories about the life of Christ. Unfortunately, little has been done to formulate the criteria for determining whether a passage is intended to be taken as factual.

As if these questions were not enough, one must also face broader philosophical concerns that relate to all history writing, whether ancient or modern. Is it possible, as a number of prominent thinkers argue, that in principle *no narrative* can give an objective account of the past?[20] Must we admit that we are

[20] Well known in this connection is Jack W. Meiland, *Scepticism and Historical Knowledge* (New York: Random House, 1965). For a recent and very clear

effectively cut off from the past? Only a minority of writers in the field accept these extreme conclusions, but the debate has forced a reconsideration of fundamental assumptions, many of which are directly relevant to the interpretive task.

In spite of all these obstacles to the historical interpretation of Scripture, historical research will continue to play a central role in the study of the Bible. But how is that role to be defined? It could be argued that, if our understanding of the Bible depends on extrabiblical data (from archaeology, for example), the believer becomes a slave to scholarly research and analysis.

Evangelicals, however, have seldom been shy to make use of archaeological discoveries; if anything, they may have been too quick to press such data into apologetic service. Some indeed would claim that conservatives tend to be unfairly selective of the material they use for their purposes. In any case, there must be some methodological boundary lines in the use (positive or negative) of extrabiblical material; more effort must be expended in formulating what those limits should be.

Of particular significance is the task of historical reconstruction. Quite often historical reconstruction implies a rejection of large portions of the biblical narrative. This inference is of course unnecessary. Any attempt to fill in historical details not explicitly stated in Scripture, such as the date of Jesus' birth or the length of his ministry, are exercises in historical reconstruction. Whenever conservatives seek to reconcile two biblical accounts that differ from each other (e.g., the nativity accounts in Matthew and Luke), they are involved in reconstructing history.[21]

Why, then, is there such wide disagreement between liberals and conservatives in this field? Does a commitment to the proposition that the Bible teaches no errors automatically place some limits on our historical investigation or analysis? If so, what precisely are those limits? Is it possible that we have

discussion of the issue, see R. F. Atkinson, *Knowledge and Explanation in History: An Introduction to the Philosophy of History* (Ithaca: Cornell University Press, 1978), chap. 2.

[21] I have made this point in "The Place of Historical Reconstruction in New Testament Criticism," in *HAC*, pp. 109–33.

merely *assumed,* but have not demonstrated, what those limits should be?

In addition to historical analysis and archaeological research, the student of ancient culture needs to pay attention to other disciplines that help to place literary documents in their proper context. Cultural anthropology, for example, has a great deal to contribute, even though biblical scholars seldom make use of it. More recently a number of researchers have placed much emphasis on sociological interpretations of the biblical books, a type of analysis that is certain to become more common in the near future.[22]

This proliferation of methods and materials makes it all the more urgent that the study of ancient culture be done within a framework that is hermeneutically coherent. The haphazard and undisciplined use of data that has characterized much biblical exegesis in the past needs to be challenged and corrected.

SCIENCE

Scientific work too involves both the collection and the *interpretation* of data. If we speak of a certain "hermeneutic" intrinsic to the scientific method, can biblical interpreters learn anything from it? The difficulties and uncertainties that attend the interpretation of literary, linguistic, and historical data may appear to us to be absent from scientific analysis. We generally think of the "hard sciences" as enjoying a measure of precision and certainty not attainable by the humanities. We realize, to be sure, that scientists sometimes formulate highly debatable theories, but we assume that such theories can and should be clearly distinguished from the facts. Thus Evangelicals often argue, and with some reason, that there is no conflict between science (i.e., "facts") and the Bible, that the conflict arises when certain modern theories are treated as scientific facts. In drawing

---

[22] See the clear descriptions by Robert R. Wilson, *Sociological Approaches to the Old Testament* (Philadelphia: Fortress, 1984), and Derek Tidball, *The Social Context of the New Testament: A Sociological Analysis* (Grand Rapids: Zondervan, 1984).

a sharp—and, as we shall see, naïve—dichotomy between fact and theory, the Evangelical is hardly alone. This approach is common and popular, even among many scientists.

In the course of the present century, however, researchers have become increasingly aware of the extent to which the observer affects the identification of the data. Werner Heisenberg's well-known uncertainty principle has been popularized frequently enough to make most of us, even if quite innocent of subatomic physics, a little more skeptical than we used to be.

But the problem is more serious. Every *description* of data necessarily involves a measure of interpretation, that is, a theoretical framework that makes the description meaningful. What persuades an individual scientist, or a community of scientists, to prefer one such theoretical framework rather than another one (e.g., a Copernican view of our planetary system rather than the Ptolemaic universe)? "The facts," we might respond. But which facts? And how many of them?

Attempting to answer questions of this sort, Thomas S. Kuhn, more than two decades ago, proposed to study the way scientific revolutions come about.[23] His analysis provoked a revolution of its own, and writers in a wide variety of disciplines have since devoted a great deal of attention to the issues he has formulated. For Kuhn, all scientific theories, even those universally accepted, are basically *paradigms,* or models, that attempt to account for as much data as possible. No theory satisfactorily explains all of the data; one always encounters *anomalies,* facts that refuse to fit the theory. Much sixteenth-century resistance to the Copernican view, for example, cannot be explained as mere dogmatism; significant pockets of the scientific community refused to give up the Ptolemaic theory, though old and shaky, for the sake of a new interpretation that could *not* explain all the facts either.

In the course of his discussion, Kuhn makes many provocative suggestions, challenging long-established ideas regarding the role of scientific discovery. He has produced some

---

[23]Thomas S. Kuhn, *The Structure of Scientific Revolutions,* 2d ed. (Chicago: University of Chicago Press, 1970; 1st ed. 1960).

fiercely loyal followers and not a few determined opponents who charge him, among other things, with espousing a dangerous form of relativism.[24] However we may respond to Kuhn's own analysis, he clearly has raised the most fundamental questions faced by the philosophy of science—indeed, by any discipline that occupies itself with the interpretation of data.

Not surprisingly, a number of theologians and exegetes have sought to appropriate these insights in their attempt to determine why different scholars or groups of scholars reach different interpretations of biblical passages. Can we understand hermeneutical changes as "paradigm shifts" of some sort? Are exegetical problems mere "anomalies" to be adjusted to the general theory? What is the connection between these discussions in the scientific community and current philosophical concerns with "preunderstanding"? And how do these concerns fit into the broader (and older) debate of whether theology itself may be regarded as a science? We may be sure that paying attention to problems in the philosophy of science will be of considerable aid in clarifying the role of biblical hermeneutics.

THEOLOGY

We have noticed, time and again in our brief survey so far, the recurrence of a basic question: What is the role of our preunderstanding in the process of interpretation? The question must now be raised once more in connection with the very discipline of which biblical exegesis is a part. Surely no one comes to the biblical text without certain *theological* presuppositions. How do those presuppositions affect our exegesis of that text?

Special attention needs to be given to the relationship between biblical exegesis and the other theological disciplines, such as biblical theology, historical and systematic theology, church history, and practical theology. The term *theological*

---

[24]The various facets of the debate can be gleaned from several collections of articles, such as Gary Gutting, ed., *Paradigms and Revolutions: Appraisals and Applications of Thomas Kuhn's Philosophy of Science* (Notre Dame: University of Notre Dame Press, 1980).

encyclopedia, though not very common nowadays, conveniently focuses on the various elements that constitute an appropriate theological curriculum.[25] Is there a coherent logic to the traditional theological encyclopedia? Can we adequately formulate how the various disciplines affect hermeneutical decisions?

A common way of expressing the relationship between the various parts of the theological encyclopedia is to view biblical criticism (including the biblical languages, historical backgrounds, literary questions, etc.) as foundational. Biblical exegesis—the detailed historico-grammatical analysis of discrete passages—builds on that foundation. The next step is biblical theology, which attempts a measure of synthesis by focusing on the distinctive teaching of individual writers (e.g., Pauline theology) or of well-defined historical periods (e.g., postexilic theology). This approach pays considerable attention to the issues of historical development and theological diversity, asking, for example, whether there is a *single* New Testament theology.

A more ambitious task is that of synthesizing the teaching of Scripture as a whole. This project is the goal of systematic theology, which requires careful attention to the development of dogma in the history of the church as well as familiarity with current cultural and philosophical concerns. Finally, there is the whole range of questions associated with practical theology: how does one communicate to present-day lay people the results of these prior disciplines? how do we present the gospel to unbelievers of various backgrounds? how does the church give expression to its faith in worship?

Anyone familiar with seminary curricula realizes that no school follows this pattern in strict sequence—as though a seminarian had to wait until the very last term to take courses in

---

[25] One of the most important works in this field is Abraham Kuyper, *Encyclopaedie der heilige godgeleerdheid,* 2d ed., 3 vols. (Kampen: J. H. Kok, 1908–9), part of the first edition of which was translated into English as *Encyclopedia of Sacred Theology: Its Principles* (New York: Scribner, 1898). A recent treatment of this topic, quite distant from Kuyper's concerns, is Edward Farley, *Theologia: The Fragmentation and Unity of Theological Education* (Philadelphia: Fortress, 1983).

practical theology! Moreover, even apart from pragmatic academic considerations, there are substantive reasons for not following a "logical" sequence of courses. The truth is that one cannot really practice, say, biblical exegesis without taking into account the concerns of systematic theology; similarly, it would be artificial to suggest that we must not or cannot address the problems posed by practical ministry until we have fully explored the area of biblical theology.

It may appear logical to require an unbiased exegesis of all the biblical passages that touch on the nature of Christ before formulating a comprehensive christology. The problem is, however, that our exegesis is always influenced by any ideas that we may consciously or unconsciously hold regarding Christ. And even if we could avoid being influenced by those ideas, we should not do so, for they provide the means to process and understand the new information that we may gather from the text. We should keep in mind that the church has made great advances in scriptural knowledge, and it would be tragic if we were to ignore all of that understanding in our own study. It is actually an illusion to think that we can somehow skip over those centuries and face the teaching of Scripture directly, with a blank mind and without the counsel of those who have gone before us.

The reader may sense something of a paradox here. Our formulation of a theological doctrine depends on the text of Scripture, yet our understanding of that text depends on our prior doctrinal knowledge. This interconnection is an aspect of the so-called hermeneutical circle, a principle that is generally accepted by scholars, though in practice one finds a good deal of resistance to it.

Many biblical scholars, for example, are deeply suspicious of systematic theology. A person who has a strong theological bent of mind is suspected of being unable to exegete the biblical text without prejudice. Indeed, to judge by comments often made at professional meetings, one might infer that the best training for biblical interpretation is to be as ignorant as possible of systematic theology. H. A. W. Meyer, the nineteenth-century scholar who could be viewed as the father of scientific commentaries, put it this way:

> The area of dogmatics and philosophy is to remain off limits for a commentary. For to ascertain the meaning the author intended to convey by his words impartially and historico-grammatically—that is the duty of the exegete. How the meaning so ascertained stands in relation to the teachings of philosophy, to what extent it agrees with the dogmas of the church or with the views of its theologians, in what way the dogmatician is to make use of it in the interest of his science—to the exegete as an exegete, all that is a matter of no concern.[26]

But no one can escape theological prejudice of one sort or another—even if it takes the form of approaching the text in an untheological fashion! And a scholar who has a keen and well-defined sense of what his or her theological commitments are may be in a better position to keep those commitments from distorting the text.

What is true of systematic theology is also true of practical theology. The needs of the pastor in the pulpit ought not to be set aside when doing biblical exegesis. One used to hear with some frequency that the exegete should be concerned only with what the text meant to the biblical writer and the original readers and that only after determining this meaning can we ask how the text applies to us today.[27]

Of course, we must be very careful not to read into the text present-day concerns that are not really there, but it i proper and even necessary to approach the Bible with a strong awareness of our needs. The problems faced in the gospe ministry often alert us to truths in Scripture that migh otherwise remain veiled to us. Proper exegesis consists largel of asking the right questions from the text, and the life of th church can provide us with those very questions.

---

[26] Quoted in Kümmel, *New Testament*, p. 111.

[27] See in this connection the famous article by Krister Stendahl, "Biblical Theology, Contemporary," *IDB* 1:418–32, esp. pp. 419–20, where he stresses how significant it was for the history of biblical criticism when the question about the meaning of the text was split into two tenses—what did/does the text mean?

But there is even more. To interpret the biblical text (or any other text, for that matter) involves a *contextual shift*. Even when I seek merely to express what Paul meant, for example, I am constrained to do so in *my* situation: with English rather than Greek, with modern rather than ancient idioms, with Western nuances rather than Middle Eastern thought forms. In other words, all forms of interpretation necessarily include a measure of *contextualization*.[28] This point is a little frightening because it appears to relativize Scripture. On the contrary, it should remind us of the relativity of our interpretation, because we are weak, limited, ignorant, and sinful. God's truth remains sure, while our perception of that truth may need to change.

Still, one must ask whether there are any limits to be drawn. The contemporary debate over contextualization has the potential for serious divisiveness in the church. Must we accept the possibility that our evangelical theology is the product of sixteenth-century thought forms and that we should be open to a distinctively African theology, for example, in which indigenous religious concepts replace Christian doctrines as we know them? What is to keep believers in foreign lands from abandoning the signs of baptism and the Lord's Supper and putting pagan customs in their place on the grounds that they are interpreting the biblical data in the light of their own context?

These questions and many others are raised by the very fact that biblical hermeneutics must take place within the framework of the broad theological task that has been given to the church. It is therefore fitting that the final volume of the series be devoted to this fundamental issue.

To return now to our original illustration, perhaps we can see a little more clearly why a knowledgeable preacher can arrive at an interpretation of Acts 5 that most of us find bizarre.

---

[28] See the useful discussion by Harvie M. Conn in his inaugural address, "The Missionary Task of Theology: A Love/Hate Relationship?" *WTJ* 45 (1983): 1–21, esp. pp. 18–21; more extensively in *Eternal Word and Changing Worlds: Theology, Anthropology, and Mission in Trialogue* (Grand Rapids: Zondervan, 1984), chap. 6.

There is no need to assume that this man was ignorant, nor even that he deliberately twisted the Scriptures for his purposes. As already suggested, the basic process by which he reached his conclusion was not essentially different from the way we normally interpret whatever we read. As we all do, this speaker had identified a particular need in the church and used a specific framework, or preunderstanding, to make sense of the biblical text.

Does this analysis mean that there can be no certainty in interpretation? One grave danger in surveying hermeneutical problems as we have just done is that of exaggerating the obstacles involved in reading a text. We need to remind ourselves that, in spite of all the difficulties we have looked at, men and women go on in their daily lives, clearly understanding most of what they read and hear. (When was the last time we argued with our friends about how to interpret the front-page story in the newspaper?)

Interpretive problems do increase, of course, when we seek to understand documents produced in earlier times and written in different languages. In the case of Scripture, the very attention that has been devoted to its interpretation has led to a very large number of exegetical suggestions. Moreover, the significance of biblical teaching for our lives makes us particularly sensitive to interpretive disagreements. It is worthwhile repeating that our interpretations, just because they are *our* interpretations, may reflect our weaknesses and sin. This fact, however, does not affect the objective certainty of God's revelation, since the truth of Scripture is independent of anyone's ability to comprehend it or willingness to receive it.

Someone may object that biblical truth is worthless to us if we cannot be sure that we have understood it. At this point we must emphasize the role of the Holy Spirit in the believer's response to divine revelation. When John tells us in his first epistle that we do not need teachers to instruct us because the Spirit anoints us with his instruction, we are thereby assured that God has not left us to our own devices in our response to revelation (1 John 2:27). Similarly, Paul states a fundamental thesis in 1 Corinthians 2:11–16 when he insists that the things of God can be understood only by those who are spiritual, that is, people who have received God's Spirit, who alone understands the things of God.

Of course, the apostles do not suggest that the Spirit guarantees the infallibility of our interpretation whenever some exegetical question is raised. Users of this series on hermeneutics ought therefore to recognize that our devoting several volumes to modern problems of interpretation does not reflect any doubt concerning the effectiveness of the Spirit's work in the believer as he or she reads the Scriptures. Our concern, rather, is to acknowledge and build upon a corresponding truth—that believers are neither perfect nor omniscient and that their desire to *grow* in the grace and knowledge of our Lord Jesus Christ must be matched by a willingness to work hard at removing whatever obstacles impede that growth.

2

OBSTACLES IN THE STUDY OF THE HISTORY OF INTERPRETATION

Before we can launch into the various disciplines outlined in the previous chapter, preliminary attention must be given to the historical roots of biblical interpretation. It must be made clear from the outset, however, that I do not intend to provide in this volume a full-blown history of biblical hermeneutics.[1] The usual chronological approach is convenient, and for certain purposes, pedagogically effective. Unfortunately, surveys of this type lead to a somewhat atomistic, item-by-item description that fails to uncover some of the more interesting and suggestive connections.

Moreover, we need to avoid the antiquarian's approach to this history—as though the concerns of ancient and medieval interpreters were oddities to be observed and then set aside. The truth is that no aspect of the current hermeneutical crisis

---

[1] The most influential work in English has been Frederic W. Farrar, *History of Interpretation* (New York: Dutton, 1886), impressive and learned—but also very misleading, as we shall see. A recent and popular description is Robert M. Grant, *A Short History of the Interpretation of the Bible,* 2d ed. with additional material by David Tracy (Philadelphia: Fortress, 1984). Most Bible dictionaries contain useful surveys. See especially *IDB* 2:718–24 (K. Grobel) and pp. 436–56 in the *Supplementary Volume* (multiauthor). D. P. Fuller, *ISBE* 2:863–74, emphasizes developments in the twentieth century. A highly regarded survey in the Continent is G. Ebeling, "Hermeneutik," *RGG* 3:242–62.

developed spontaneously without any prior connections. The problems *we* face can be dealt with satisfactorily only if we recognize that they are not altogether new, that many of the old controversies (silly though they may look to us) are not substantially different from those that divide contemporary readers of the Bible.

Of particular importance is the popular assumption that the Christian church, through most of its history, has misread the Bible. Did an invalid hermeneutics reign among interpreters while crucial theological issues were being decided? Before we can address this fundamental question, it may be useful to review briefly the common perception of the history of biblical interpretation.

THE USUAL CONCEPTION

A typical survey of the church's interpretation of the Bible might take this form:

The origins of biblical interpretation are to be found within Judaism, which provided the context for different approaches. First, among sectarians, such as the people of the Dead Sea Scrolls, biblical interpretation had a marked eschatological note. Passage after passage in the Old Testament was understood as referring to the end times, which were in the process of being fulfilled in the context of the Qumran community.

Second, among the rabbis, whose approach developed into mainstream Judaism, exegesis consisted of mechanical and artificial rules that paid virtually no attention to the context of the biblical passages. In the more extreme cases, such as the methods of Akiba, an irrational literalism and obsession with trivial details led to wholesale distortions of the Scriptures.

Third, in the Jewish Hellenistic world, particularly Alexandria, Greek allegorical methods used in the interpretation of Homeric legends were applied to the Bible. Best known among Jewish allegorizers is Philo, who rejected literalism on the grounds that it led to blasphemous and even immoral interpretations. For him, biblical narratives, if interpreted literally, were at best irrelevant: we must discover the underlying meaning of these passages, which usually corresponds to the best in Greek philosophy.

In contrast to these approaches, the New Testament shows a remarkably balanced method of interpretation. There may be a very few examples of allegorization (perhaps Gal. 4:21–31 and Heb. 7:1–10), but even these passages are rather moderate in comparison with Philo. Again, some rabbinic rules of interpretation seem to be reflected in various New Testament passages, but apostolic exegesis shows considerable respect for the Old Testament context. And while one must recognize that the apostles, like the Qumran community, used an eschatological hermeneutics, their approach was built upon a distinctively christological foundation.

As we move to the postapostolic period, the picture changes dramatically. Since the Qumran community had been destroyed in A.D. 70, its peculiar exegesis was basically unknown in the Christian church. Moreover, rabbinic methods had little impact on the Gentile church, partly because very few Christians were familiar with Hebrew and partly because anti-Jewish feelings prevented any significant communication (there were of course some important exceptions, such as Origen and Jerome, but even they did not adopt rabbinic exegesis).

Allegorical exegesis, however, was something else. Since Philo had written in Greek, his works were accessible to the Gentile church. Moreover, Christians were faced with the need to confront Greek culture, and Philo appeared to provide a way of doing so in an intellectually responsible way. Origen in particular made the allegorical method a central feature of his exegesis and his theology, and his influence was to be felt for many centuries.

To be sure, important Christian leaders such as Tertullian rejected any attempt to mix the gospel with Greek philosophy. And in Antioch an exegetical approach was developed during the fourth century that was self-consciously opposed to Origen and that could be described as "grammatico-historical," if only in a limited way. (Important representatives of this school were John Chrysostom and Theodore of Mopsuestia.) As a whole, however, the allegorical interpretation was adopted by the church and hardly anything of exegetical value was produced during the Middle Ages.

Fortunately, the Reformation came along. Thanks in part to the Renaissance, which resurrected an interest in linguistic and historical investigation, the Reformers attacked the allegorical method as a major source of the many evils that had developed in the church. Many new commentaries, particularly those of John Calvin, inaugurated a new epoch in the interpretation of Scripture.

These advances were to some extent nullified by seventeenth-century orthodox theologians who reintroduced a scholastic mentality, but the eighteenth-century Enlightenment finally brought in a truly scientific approach to the interpretation of the Bible. While some scholars took matters to an extreme and their rationalism was damaging to the Christian faith, by and large the grammatico-historical method of exegesis established itself firmly during the nineteenth century and continues to be used in our day.

So much for the usual description. Depending on the theological stance of the person reporting this history, some aspects and details may differ here and there, particularly in the evaluation of post-Enlightenment scholarship. Generally speaking, however, our brief survey reflects rather accurately the usual understanding of the church's interpretation of the Scriptures. Unfortunately, there are some serious problems with this understanding.

OBJECTIONS

In the first place, our survey did not go back far enough, since it paid no attention to the earliest stage of biblical interpretation, namely, the Old Testament itself. The books of the Old Testament were written over a very long period of time, and it would be surprising if the later books made no use of the earlier ones. No one has denied that various kinds of references of this sort exist, but only recently have scholars focused on this issue with a view to drawing hermeneutical inferences.[2]

---

[2] See esp. Michael A. Fishbane, *Biblical Interpretation in Ancient Israel* (Oxford: Clarendon, 1985), for the most thorough treatment of this question. Much

This field of study presents us with a few problems, not the least of which is the uncertainty we face when trying to establish the relative date of some of the documents. In certain cases—particularly the date of the Pentateuch—disagreement among scholars creates a serious obstacle, but we still have a number of clear instances in which later Old Testament writers have used, expanded, or otherwise applied earlier passages.

We might take, for instance, Jacob's prophecy that the scepter would not depart from Judah before *šlh* should come (Gen. 49:10). Is that Hebrew word the proper name *Shiloh,* as some translations have it? Or should we render the clause as the NIV does, "until he comes to whom it belongs"? In favor of the latter option is an apparent reference to this prophecy by Ezekiel, who predicts the removal of the crown from the prince of Israel and adds: "It will not be restored until he comes to whom it rightfully belongs; to him I will give it" (Ezek. 21:27).

One can find many other passages that almost surely depend on earlier material. An especially fruitful example is the way 1–2 Chronicles retells the historical material found in the Books of Samuel and Kings.[3] Even in such clear instances, however, it is seldom easy to identify a particular principle or technique that we can readily apply to our own exegetical efforts. Much work remains to be done in this area.

A second problem with the usual approach to the history of interpretation is the strongly negative note with which the subject is treated. Farrar's famous *History* is little more than a compilation of errors. Already in the preface he warns us about "the apparently negative character of much that is here dwelt upon," and in the first chapter he states his thesis thus:

> The task before us is in some respects a melancholy one. We shall pass in swift review many centuries of exegesis, and shall be compelled to see that they were, in the main, centuries during which the interpretation of Scripture has been dominated by

briefer but also helpful is James L. Kugel and Rowan A. Greer, *Early Biblical Interpretation* (Library of Early Christianity; Philadelphia: Westminster, 1986), pt. 1.

[3] See the study by Raymond B. Dillard, "The Chronicler's Solomon," *WTJ* 43 (1980–81): 289–300.

unproven theories, and overladen by untenable results. We shall
see that these theories have often been affiliated to each other,
and augmented at each stage by the superaddition of fresh
theories no less mistaken. Exegesis has often darkened the true
meaning of Scripture, not evolved or elucidated it.

Near the end of that first chapter he tells us that "the
misinterpretation of Scripture must be reckoned among the
gravest calamities of Christendom." Much of the blame goes to
the Septuagint, whose "intentional variations may be counted
by scores, and their unintentional errors by hundreds; and alike
their errors and their variations were in a multitude of instances
accepted by Christian interpreters as the infallible word of
God."[4] Although Farrar has some complimentary words here
and there (particularly with reference to the Antiochenes and the
Reformers), one is hard-pressed to find much in that history
that would help us in our exegetical work—except possibly to
avoid a multitude of errors.

Apart from the general negativism of the standard
approaches, it is important to point out the particular areas that
come under heavy attack. One of the main objects of derision is
rabbinic exegesis. Here is Farrar's opinion of the Talmud:

> But it may be said, without fear of refutation, that, apart from a
> few moral applications and ritual inferences in matters absolutely
> unimportant, for every one text on which it throws the smallest
> glimmer of light, there are hundreds which it inexcusably
> perverts and misapplies. . . . [Hillel's rule known as Gezerah
> Shawa] furnished an excuse for masses of the most absurd
> conclusions. . . . Hillel was personally a noble Rabbi; yet by his
> seven rules he became the founder of Talmudism, with all its
> pettiness, its perversion of the letter of the Scripture which it
> professed to worship, and its ignorance of the spirit, of which no
> breath seemed to breathe over its valley of dry bones.[5]

---

[4]Farrar, *History*, pp. xi, xviii, 8–9, 39, 122. A similar attitude can be found in
Samuel Davidson, *Sacred Hermeneutics: Developed and Applied* (Edinburgh:
T. Clark, 1843), esp. p. 187. Grant, *Short History*, is better, but even he has
some unnecessarily harsh remarks about Barnabas, Justin, and Protestant
orthodoxy (pp. 41, 45, 97).

[5]Ibid., pp. 10, 20, 22; see also pp. 50 and 88.

Farrar believes that Christian exegesis, fortunately, did not share the particular perversions of the rabbis, but his introduction to patristic interpretation is not encouraging either:

> The history of exegesis thus far has been in great measure a history of aberrations. If we turn to the Fathers with the hope that now at last we shall enter the region of unimpeachable methods and certain applications, we shall be disappointed. . . . [Though admittedly one can find much that is valuable in the Fathers,] their exegesis in the proper sense of the word needs complete revision both in its principles and in its details.[6]

The main culprit behind patristic misinterpretation is of course Origen of Alexandria, who gave respectability to Philo's allegorical method. With regard to Philo's approach, Farrar had already stated: "It must be said quite plainly and without the least circumlocution that it is absolutely baseless. . . . his exegesis is radically false. It darkens what is simple and fails to explain what is obscure." Origen was hardly successful in improving upon Philo. What Origen regarded as exegetical "proofs" were nothing "but the after-thoughts devised in support of an unexamined tradition. They could not have had a particle of validity for any logical or independent mind."[7]

In addition to rabbinic exegesis and the allegorical method, a third object of Farrar's criticism is medieval scholasticism. We should note that, during the past few decades, specialists have developed a much more positive appreciation of

---

[6] Ibid., p. 162; on p. 165 he describes their interpretation as consisting of "a chaos" of diverse elements. David C. Steinmetz is probably correct when he views Farrar's book as "a triumph of what the late Sir Herbert Butterfield of Cambridge called 'Whig' historiography. Farrar admires about the past precisely those elements in it most like the present and regards the present, indeed, as the inevitable culmination of all that was best in the past" ("John Calvin on Isaiah 6: A Problem in the History of Exegesis," *Int* 36 [1982]: p. 169).

[7] Ibid., pp. 153, 191. Farrar concludes that the very foundations of Origen's "exegetic system are built upon the sand" (p. 201). Even St. Augustine, for all his greatness, made little advance in interpretive method. For Farrar, Augustine's exegesis "is marked by the most glaring defects. Almost as many specimens of prolix puerility and arbitrary perversion can be adduced from his pages as from those of his least gifted predecessors" (p. 236).

the Middle Ages than was the case in Farrar's generation. Nowadays many scholars are ready to argue, for example, that "the medieval hermeneutical tradition . . . can be characterized as an authentic attempt to establish the *sensus literalis* of Scripture as its principal meaning, and to give it a theologically normative role in the formation of Christian theology."[8] In Farrar's opinion, on the other hand, the Schoolmen were "paralysed by vicious methods, traditional errors, and foregone conclusions," while their exegesis was "radically defective—defective in fundamental principles, and rife on every page of it with all sorts of erroneous details."[9]

Behind all of this invective is Farrar's conviction that, first, many of these errors are still to be found "here and there, unexorcised, in modern commentaries," and, second, that the main cause of these old exegetical perversions is the theory of "verbal dictation."[10] Farrar's own view of inspiration, incidentally, helps explain why he does not feel threatened by the miserable failure of the church in interpreting the Bible. In his opinion, inspiration assures only that the message of salvation, broadly understood, is preserved in Scripture: "the Bible is not so much a revelation as the *record* of revelation, and the inmost and most essential truths which it contains have happily been placed above the reach of Exegesis to injure."[11]

[8]James Samuel Preus, *From Shadow to Promise: Old Testament Interpretation from Augustine to Young Luther* (Cambridge, Mass.: Harvard University Press, Belknap, 1969), p. 3. For a renewed appreciation of medieval exegesis, we are largely indebted to Beryl Smalley's work, particularly *The Study of the Bible in the Middle Ages,* 2d ed. (Oxford: Blackwell, 1952).

[9]Farrar, *History,* pp. 267, 302.

[10]Ibid., pp. xii, xx, 190, 283, 430, etc. Farrar shows considerable confusion in dealing with this matter, as can be seen particularly in the footnotes on p. xx. In the first place, he equates "verbal dictation" with the doctrine of infallibility. Moreover, he refers with apparent approval to Tholuck's claim that this view is no earlier than the seventeenth century—even though such a claim blatantly contradicts his repeated attribution of that doctrine to many early historical figures, such as Philo, the rabbis, Athenagoras, Tertullian, and Origen (see pp. 148, 152, 162, 171, 177, 190).

[11]Ibid., p. xiv; cf. also p. 303.

TOWARD A POSITIVE EVALUATION

Whatever we may think of Farrar's doctrine of Scripture, it is difficult to accept the thoroughgoing negativism with which he recounts the history of interpretation. After all, the individuals he discusses were believers seeking to make sense of God's Word, with a view to obeying the divine will. Are we to suppose that their efforts were, with the rarest of exceptions, virtually fruitless? Must we really think that, prior to the development of modern exegesis, the church lacked the Spirit's guidance?

Farrar appears to suggest that only two options are available to us: Either we accept modern exegetical methods and reject a good 95 percent of pre-eighteenth-century biblical interpretation, or else we condemn ourselves to adopting countless errors. Perhaps, however, we can be genuinely critical of shortcomings on the part of the Fathers and still learn something more positive than how to avoid their errors. Surely, it is conceivable that their failures may have been counterbalanced by other factors that can help us to formulate a valid hermeneutical approach. David C. Steinmetz comments that the answer to Farrar is not to point out examples of "modern" exegesis in the Middle Ages (or howlers in modern times): "The principal value of precritical exegesis is that it is not modern exegesis; it is alien, strange, sometimes even, from our perspective, comic and fantastical."[12]

In any case, we can hardly claim to have developed a satisfactory approach *if our exegesis is in essence incompatible with the way God's people have read the Scriptures throughout the centuries.* A genuine effort must be made to view the history of interpretation in a more positive light than is usually done. The reason why this is so necessary is not difficult to understand. Most believers even today lack the specialized skills that characterize modern "scientific" exegesis. Since they therefore read the Scriptures in a "nonscientific" way, they are basically

---

[12]Steinmetz, "John Calvin," p. 170.

in the same position as earlier Christians who lived in a prescientific period.

Moreover, one may argue that scholarly exegesis, though it rightly uses highly specialized methods, fails to provide proper guidance if it disregards the simple or instinctive response to Scripture on the part of lay readers. It may indeed appear impossible for modern biblical scholarship to discover any relationship between the historical method and the quasi-allegorical approach that is standard fare among lay Christians. The failure to confront this dilemma head-on, however, can only lead to an unbearable divorce between scholarly work and common piety.

There is, in addition to these concerns, a profound intellectual problem with the usual negative analysis. Take the case of Origen. It is agreed on all sides that Origen was one of the brightest luminaries in his day—not only within the Christian community, but even in the context of the whole cultural scene in the third century. How, then, does one account for his constructing a hermeneutical system that draws bitter scorn from moderns?

Origen's allegorical method was not some peripheral concern that we might disregard as an uncharacteristic quirk. Quite the contrary, it belonged at the center of his theological thinking. If, as Farrar claimed, his exegetical proofs had no "particle of validity for any logical or independent mind," are we not compelled to conclude that Origen's mind was neither logical nor independent? And is not that conclusion clear evidence that we have failed to solve, or maybe even to identify, the problem?

If my own experience as a seminarian was at all typical, most students find Origen a difficult, distant, unhelpful personality. One can find many objectionable elements in his writings and few that appear genuinely constructive. The more one reflects on the subsequent history of interpretation, however, the more one becomes aware of the significance of Origen's thought. He anticipated virtually every substantive hermeneutical debate in the history of the church, including some that have persisted to this day. It would no doubt be an exaggeration to say that the history of biblical interpretation consists of a series of footnotes to Origen, but there is enough truth in that remark to make us sit up and take notice. Accordingly, the chapters that follow pay a great deal of attention to Origen's writings. Even if we decide to reject his answers, it is impossible to avoid his questions.

Now what Origen's questions most clearly reveal is that the task of biblical interpretation seems to pull the believer in several different directions. I propose in this volume to study the history of interpretation precisely in that light. My thesis is simply that this history is characterized by the church's appreciation, sometimes implicit rather than consciously formulated, that we face a series of difficult "tensions" in our reading of Scripture:[13]

- The Bible is divine, yet it has come to us in human form.
- The commands of God are absolute, yet the historical context of the writings appears to relativize certain elements.
- The divine message must be clear, yet many passages seem ambiguous.
- We are dependent only on the Spirit for instruction, yet scholarship is surely necessary.
- The Scriptures seem to presuppose a literal and historical reading, yet we are also confronted by the figurative and nonhistorical (e.g., the parables).
- Proper interpretation requires the interpreter's personal freedom, yet some degree of external, corporate authority appears imperative.
- The objectivity of the biblical message is essential, yet

---

[13] I use quotation marks here to alert the reader to a certain ambiguity in the word *tension*. I am using the term not in any sophisticated fashion but in a simple, popular sense. As we seek to understand the Scriptures, we sometimes feel as though contradictory responses are expected of us. Besides such feelings, we also may experience intellectual frustration. But the believer knows well that these difficulties arise from our own ignorance and sin.

our presuppositions seem to inject a degree of subjectivity into the interpretive process.

The attempt to hold these seeming polarities in tension is the principle that brings unity to the great diversity of problems surrounding the history of biblical interpretation. It may well be that the one great aim in our own interpretation of Scripture must be that of resisting the temptation to eliminate the tensions, to emphasize certain features of the Bible at the expense of others.

DIVINE OR HUMAN?

The first item listed above—the Bible as both divine and human—constitutes the most basic question of all. Strictly speaking, it is not so much a hermeneutical question as it is one of theology, even though, as we shall see in the course of our discussions, one can hardly divorce doctrine from interpretation. Since the present book is not intended to serve as a text for Christian theology, I consider here only briefly the doctrine of biblical inspiration.[14]

But treat it we must, for the relationship between the divine and human elements of Scripture directly affects how we handle every other item on the list. I do not say, of course, that our view of the character of Scripture automatically determines whether we will, for example, take prophetic passages in a literal or nonliteral way. Nevertheless, it is hardly possible to formulate a coherent set of hermeneutical principles unless one takes fully into account how those principles relate to the essential nature of the documents being interpreted.

Origen's most important theological work, *On First Principles,* consists of four books, the last of which is devoted to

---

[14] In addition to Hodge and Warfield, *Inspiration,* note the important articles by Warfield brought together in *The Inspiration and Authority of the Bible,* ed. Samuel G. Craig (Philadelphia: Presbyterian & Reformed, 1948), esp. chaps. 2–4. One of the most recent and learned discussions, particularly valuable in addressing contemporary objections to Evangelicalism, is Carl F. H. Henry, *God, Revelation, and Authority,* 6 vols. (Waco, Tex.: Word, 1976–83), esp. vol. 4, chap. 6.

principles of biblical interpretation. Not surprisingly, the first chapter of that book deals with inspiration, and Origen intends to establish the divine character of Scripture as the foundation for hermeneutics. Origen develops his argument by appealing to fulfilled prophecy, the success of the apostles, and other types of evidence. As he approaches the end of the chapter, he writes:

> Now when we thus briefly demonstrate the divine nature of Jesus and use the words spoken in prophecy about him, we demonstrate at the same time that the writings which prophesy about him are divinely inspired and that the words which announce his sojourning here and his teaching were spoken with all power and authority and that this is the reason why they have prevailed over the elect people taken from among the nations.[15]

Origen also appeals to the reader's subjective response: "And he who approaches the prophetic words with care and attention will feel from his very reading a trace of their divine inspiration and will be convinced by his own feelings that the words which are believed by us to be from God are not the compositions of men." He realizes, of course, that not everyone who reads the Bible acknowledges it as divine, and so in section 7 he draws an analogy based on the failure of many people to detect God's existence through the works of providence:

> But just as providence is not abolished because of our ignorance, at least not for those who have once rightly believed in it, so neither is the divine character of scripture, which extends through all of it, abolished because our weakness cannot discern in every sentence the hidden splendour of its teachings, concealed under a poor and humble style.[16]

The very last clause just quoted, we may note, entails a recognition that there is *more* to be said about Scripture than that it is divine. The human character of Scripture does not concern Origen at this point (in fact, he nowhere deliberately reflects on the implications of that fact with the same thoroughness he displays in treating the Bible's divine character). As a result, he

---

[15] Origen, *Origen on First Principles,* trans. G. W. Butterworth (New York: Harper & Row, 1966; orig. 1936) 4. 1. 6, p. 264.

[16] Ibid., 4. 1. 7, pp. 265, 267.

may appear to disregard or even ignore it. We have already seen his comment that the biblical writings "are not the compositions of men." In section 4. 2. 2 he identifies himself with "those who believe that the sacred books *are not the works of men,* but that they were composed and have come down to us as a result of the inspiration of the Holy Spirit."[17] It would be easy to multiply quotations from Origen's extensive writings that suggest he viewed the Scriptures as exclusively divine.

The very nature of his scholarly labors, however, belies such a conclusion. His concern with textual and philological details makes sense only on the assumption that he recognized the important role played by language and other human factors.[18] Our discussion in subsequent chapters should make clear that Origen's primary concern with what *God* says in Scripture does not necessarily preclude a commitment to find out what its human authors meant.

At any rate, we must acknowledge that heavy emphasis on the divine character of Scripture has characterized most of the history of interpretation. One reason for this emphasis, of course, is simply that some of the human features of the Bible are patent and undeniable: it was written by real-life historical individuals rather than appearing from nowhere, it was written in human languages rather than in some unknown angelic tongue, and so on. In other words, the church has not had to deal with people who deny, at least in any conscious or explicit form, the fact that there is a human side to the Scriptures, whereas it has had to respond to many who deny their divine origin.

One must admit, however, that in actual practice Origen

---

[17]Ibid. 4. 2. 2, p. 272, my emphasis.

[18]How this recognition affected Origen's practice of interpretation may be illustrated from the preface to *On First Principles.* Answering an objection based on a passage from *The Teaching of Peter* (a writing that Origen did not accept as inspired, though he granted its inspiration for the sake of the argument), he stated: "And the words must be understood in the sense intended by the author of that writing" (section 8 of the preface, p. 5). We are not concerned here primarily with Origen's critical labors, the best known of which was the Hexapla. It may be worth pointing out, however, that he saw such works, not as ends in themselves, but as the first steps in understanding the *divine* message.

and most of the interpreters who followed him in the ancient
and medieval periods tended to disregard the human (and
therefore historical) aspects of the text because of their commitment to its divine character. This tendency led to many
interpretive errors, such as the full-scale development of
allegorical exegesis, which usually focused on the divine
meaning "behind" the human words, a matter that we consider
in chapter 3.

The Renaissance witnessed a renewed interest in the
historical character of ancient writings, including the Bible. Its
effect on the Reformers, particularly Calvin, was direct. It must
not be thought that the Reformers downplayed the divine
origin of Scripture; their concern with the "plain" meaning of
the Bible (that is, the meaning intended by the *human* author, as
that sense can be plainly determined by the literary and
historical context) did not entail a change in their view of
inspiration. Significantly, Calvin at times so stressed the divine
character of Scripture that he, like Origen, appeared to deny its
humanity: "not the word of the apostles but of God himself; not
a voice born on earth but one descended from heaven."[19]
Although the arguments he used to defend the doctrine of
inspiration marked a substantive advance over previous discussions, they have much in common with those of Origen.
Calvin's commitment to the "paradox" that the Bible is both
divine and human is no doubt a major reason why moderns can
appeal to some of his statements as evidence that he did not
believe in verbal inspiration, while other comments make
absolutely no sense unless he did.[20]

Without denying the distinctiveness of the Reformers'
contribution, then, we do well to remember their basic sense of

[19] John Calvin, *Institutes of the Christian Religion,* ed. John T. McNeill, trans.
Ford Lewis Battles (Library of Christian Classics 20; Philadelphia: Westminster,
1967) 4. 11. 1, p. 1213. See section 1. 6–8 for his defense of inspiration.

[20] In my opinion, one can hardly doubt that Calvin's view of the authority of
Scripture corresponds in all essential respects to that of Warfield. See John
Murray, *Calvin on Scripture and Divine Sovereignty* (Philadelphia: Presbyterian &
Reformed, 1960), esp. chap. 1. The apparent inconsistency of expression is
more remarkable in Jerome; see Farrar, *History,* pp. 230–31.

continuity with earlier centuries, at least with respect to the divine character of Scripture. The Reformation, of course, also retained the medieval concern for application, though it sought to bind application to the clear meaning of the text.

The rise of the critical method, on the other hand, marked a radical change in the way students of the Bible approached the text. To begin with, there was a tendency to view exegesis as an end in itself. And for the first time in the history of the church, scholars who professed some form of Christian commitment argued that the Bible was to be understood just like any other book. In a sense, of course, the best exegetes had always attempted to interpret the Bible in this way, that is, according to the normal rules of language, paying attention to logic, literary conventions, historical data, and so on.

Now, however, interpreters argued that the Bible must be subjected to the same kind of full-blown *criticism* that one might apply to any human writing, even if the analysis leads to a negative assessment of its value at any point.[21] Proponents of this method did not agree with each other concerning whether the Bible could still be regarded as divine (and if so, in what sense), but they did agree that such a factor could not play a role in its interpretation. The whole conception of biblical authority, therefore, if not blatantly abandoned, was drastically altered: an individual's reason first had to make a judgment regarding the validity of a biblical statement or injunction before one could believe it.

The development of biblical hermeneutics during the past two centuries cannot possibly be separated from the application of critical tools to the biblical text. This factor raises a series of major problems. In the first place, the interpretation of the Bible now appears to require expertise in a number of highly

---

[21] More accurately, it was claimed that critical exegesis should not consist in value judgments. The eighteenth-century scholar K. A. G. Keil, for example, argued that proper biblical interpretation could not ask whether the text is right or wrong. This restriction, however, meant that one must disregard inspiration (see Kümmel, *New Testament,* p. 108; cf. p. 110 on L. I. Ruckert). In other words, the divine element was excluded, and with it the possibility that the Scriptures were always reliable.

specialized subdisciplines. Does this qualification put the Scriptures out of the reach of most believers? Can we possibly claim that the Bible is *clear*? (We consider this issue in chapter 4.)

Second, we are faced with a new and most difficult dilemma. On the one hand, many of the critical tools used by modern scholarship are patently consistent with a high view of scriptural authority; that is, scholars with strong evangelical convictions can plainly make use of, say, textual criticism without compromising their view of biblical inspiration. On the other hand, most of these tools have taken shape in the context of blatant unbelief. The point here is not merely that some unbelievers have had a hand in their development but that such a development assumed, in the very nature of the case, that the Scriptures must be fallible. Are these tools therefore inherently "tainted," whether we realize it or not, and therefore unusable by anyone committed to the full authority of the Bible? Some conservative Christians would answer this question affirmatively. For that matter, liberal scholars often accuse Evangelicals of inconsistency in holding on to inerrancy while making use of critical tools.

> Troeltsch poured scorn on those of his contemporaries who attacked the historical method as a manifestation of unbelief while employing something like it to vindicate the truth of their own views. The method, he claimed, did not grow from an abstract theory, nor could one ignore the cumulative significance of its extraordinary results. "Whoever lends it a finger must give it a hand." Nor could the critical method be regarded as a neutral thing. It could not be appropriated by the church with only a bit of patchwork here and there on the seamless garment of belief. "Once the historical method is applied to the Biblical science and church history," he wrote, "it is a leaven that alters everything and, finally, bursts apart the entire structure of theological methods employed until the present."[22]

***

[22] Van Austin Harvey, *The Historian and the Believer: The Morality of Historical Knowledge and Christian Belief* (New York: Macmillan, 1966), p. 5. From a somewhat different angle, James Barr has been particularly anxious to show that Evangelicals have a very equivocal approach to scholarship. See his *Fundamentalism* (London: SCM, 1977), esp. chap. 5. Barr observes, "The deservedly high reputation of some conservative scholarship rests to a large extent on the degree

Third, and most directly relevant to our present concerns, it is now claimed that a full acceptance of the critical method, with its assumption of biblical fallibility, is the only approach that does justice to the humanity of Scripture. Ironically, conservatives become the theological felons, charged with a form of *docetism,* an ancient heresy that denied the true humanity of Christ.

The analogy between Scripture and the twofold nature of Christ, though very popular in some circles, suffers from some deep ambiguities.[23] Even if it did not, however, one wonders how the charge of docetism contributes to the discussion, other than by affecting the objectivity of the debate through the "slur" factor. Strangely, I have never heard anyone accused of *Arianism* in his or her view of Scripture, though it could be argued that, once we abandon the doctrine of infallibility, there is no meaningful way in which we can speak of the divine character of the Bible.

The last point can best be illustrated by referring to a World Council of Churches study report on biblical authority presented in 1971. Heavily influenced by Karl Barth's theology, the members of the committee were reluctant to base the authority of Scripture on the notion of inspiration, and so they pointed rather to "the experience in which the message of the Bible proves itself authoritative." To their credit, they went on to ask the embarrassing question:

> If the assertion that the Bible is inspired is a conclusion drawn from actual encounter with God through the Bible, the question arises as to why this should only be true of the Bible. . . . Indeed, why should we not also speak of inspiration in the case of today's preaching which can also lead to an encounter with God and thus prove itself inspired in the same way as happens with the Bible?

---

to which it *fails* to be conservative in the sense that the conservative evangelical public desiderate" (p. 128).

[23] For a perceptive discussion, see G. C. Berkouwer, *Holy Scripture* (Studies in Dogmatics; Grand Rapids: Eerdmans, 1975), chap. 7. See also D. A. Carson, "Recent Developments in the Doctrine of Scripture," in *HAC,* pp. 5–48, esp. his criticism of Bruce Vawter on pp. 26–28.

It would certainly be difficult to think of a more fundamental question than that of the uniqueness of scriptural authority. The fact that this notion had lost all meaning for the committee may be inferred from their remarkable response: "Obviously a clearer explanation is required as to whether and in what sense God has bound Himself through the Spirit to the Bible in its entirety."[24] To paraphrase: We have no idea in what way the Bible is unique.

The position taken in this book is that error is not inherent to humanity—it may be true that to err is human, but it is most certainly untrue that to be human is to err! A human being can (and often does) utter sentences that contain no errors or falsehoods (e.g., "Hitler is dead" or, under the appropriate circumstances, "I saw my mother yesterday"). Accordingly, we do not jeopardize the humanity of Scripture if we say that all it affirms is true. At the same time, we may readily acknowledge that an evangelical view of Scripture has led many to downplay its human character—if not in theory, certainly in the practice of interpretation.

As with Calvin, our attempt to affirm both the divine and human sides of Scripture will almost inevitably lead to statements that appear inconsistent. This problem only reminds us of our finiteness. But the alternative would be to deny one or the other element, which we dare not do.

---

[24] Ellen Flesseman-van Leer, ed., *The Bible: Its Authority and Interpretation in the Ecumenical Movement* (Faith and Order Paper 99; Geneva: World Council of Churches, 1980), pp. 54–55.

3

LITERAL OR FIGURATIVE?

The concept of figurative language can encompass a rather wide variety of phenomena. Consider the following examples of biblical interpretation:

1. The promise that "new wine will drip from the mountains" (Amos 9:13) is a figure of speech indicating the abundance of divine blessings at the end time.
2. When the Bible speaks of God's "eyes" or his "mouth," we are not to deduce that God has a body; human qualities are being attributed to him so that we may better understand the biblical message.
3. Isaac was a historical character, but in Galatians 4:21–31 Paul views him as a type of those who are born by the Spirit of God.
4. The statement "Out of Egypt I called my son" (Hos. 11:1) refers to the people of Israel, but Matthew sees in it a fuller meaning that applies to Jesus' childhood (Matt. 2:15).
5. The Old Testament prophecies regarding the restoration of Israel should be understood in a spiritual sense, referring to the Christian church.
6. The story of Jonah is probably not historical: it should be viewed as a parable intended to teach a lesson.

7. Jesus' changing the water to wine at the wedding in Cana (John 2:1–11) symbolizes the need for those who are weak like water to be changed and become steadfast like wine.

The first of these examples is a simple case of *metaphor*; the second is a special type of metaphor known as *anthropomorphism*. With the third example we meet an interpretive method known as *typology*, the view that certain historical characters or events in some way prefigure others corresponding to them in a later period. These three instances of interpretation are not normally disputed among biblical students.

The others are more controversial. Number 4 expresses a concept known as *sensus plenior*, which indicates that an Old Testament writer, for example, may be quite unaware of a deeper meaning found in his own writing. The fifth, an instance of so-called *spiritualizing*, divides some important segments of Christianity. We may refer to number 6 as an instance of *dehistoricizing* interpretation, while the last example illustrates *allegorizing*.

In this chapter I use the term *figurative* in a very broad sense to include all of these approaches. It may appear at first blush that I am thereby mixing apples and oranges. Was not the typological method, for example, developed in conscious opposition to allegorizing?[1] The answer to this type of question

---

[1] I refer here to the Antiochene school, with which we shall deal below. We may note at this point Hans W. Frei, *The Eclipse of Biblical Narrative: A Study in Nineteenth Century Hermeneutics* (New Haven: Yale University Press, 1974). On p. 2 he identifies typology as figuration, yet at the same time as "a natural extension of literal interpretation. It was literalism at the level of the whole biblical story and thus of the depiction of the whole of historical reality. Figuration was at once a literary and a historical procedure." Later on, however, as a result of changes in the way scholars viewed narrative, "figural sense came to be something like the opposite of literal sense" (p. 7). More to the point, the ancients did not see a clear distinction between allegory and typology. Augustine, *On Christian Doctrine* 3. 11 (*NPNF* 2:561) identifies "allegorical or enigmatical" as "the kind of expression properly called *figurative*." Wolfgang A. Bienert, *«Allegoria» und «Anagoge» bei Didymus dem Blinden von Alexandria* (PTS 13; Berlin: W. de Gruyter, 1972), pp. 42–43, argues that, both in the Greek church and in the Latin church, *allegoria* could refer to either allegorical or

is that all of the approaches listed above share one fundamental feature: they recognize that, at certain points in the biblical text, there appears to be "something more" than is immediately apparent. This phenomenon is not peculiar to Scripture. In the reading of any text, one is always in danger of interpreting statements in a "woodenly literal" fashion.

It may help to clarify our problem if we describe two approaches that seem to represent extreme opposites: Aquila's literalistic translation of the Old Testament into Greek and Origen's full-blown allegorical method. Moderns routinely caricature Aquila and Origen as exemplifying puerile and nearly irrational methods of exegesis.

Seminary teachers have learned that they can get a quick laugh in Hebrew class by informing their sophisticated students that Aquila translated the particle *'et* in Genesis 1:1 (where it simply signals the direct object) as though it were the preposition meaning "with." And what respectable church history professor has allowed Origen and his "wild" interpretations to escape unscathed?[2] Surely Aquila and Origen are viewed as two great examples of how *not* to exegete. Their hermeneutical approaches are thought to represent the worst that prescientific, ancient exegesis had to offer.

This analysis is much too simple, however. As pointed out in chapter 2, Origen's intellectual gifts were second to none. Does it make sense that he would build his theological system on a method of exegesis that is so patently illogical? Similarly, it is apparent that Aquila was no fool, that his strange renderings reflect not ignorance of the Hebrew language but rather a self-conscious approach to a method of interpretation closely related to that of Rabbi Akiba.

At the very least, we need to attempt an explanation for this anomaly. What led intelligent people to develop such

typological exegesis. On the varied uses of *tropikos* ("figurative"), see Theodoret de Cyr, *Commentaire sur Isaïe*, 3 vols., ed. and trans. Jean-Noel Guinot (Sources chrétiennes 276, 295, 315; Paris: Cerf, 1980–84), 1:70–71.

[2]For an entertaining list of insults, see Henri de Lubac, *Histoire et Esprit: L'intelligence de l'Écriture d'après Origène* (Théologie 16; Paris: Aubier, 1950), pp. 13ff.

methods and to consider them important? That question needs to be answered before we can dismiss their approaches as having absolutely no value for us. As Wiles puts it, we can hardly sit in judgment of Origen, since "the fundamental problem remains unsolved."[3]

Another reason why this whole issue is not a simple one is that neither of the two approaches is used exclusively by underprivileged ancients and uneducated modern believers. For example, the difficult question concerning whether Bible translations (or translations of any text, for that matter) should be "literal" has not been satisfactorily resolved.[4] It is all very well to point to the results of modern linguistics and its demonstration that literal translations are not necessarily accurate. On that basis, translations that follow the principle of "formal correspondence" (e.g., the NASB) are ridiculed as more or less obscurantist and unscientific. Critics will then suggest that literalistic translators are ignorant of modern linguistics or that their view of verbal inspiration disqualifies them from proper translation work.

Now one must admit that a "dynamic equivalence," rather than "formal correspondence," approach to translation is more likely to transmit the main point of a text clearly and reliably to the reader. It is also undeniable, however, that the former approach, no less than the latter, entails almost inevitably the loss of certain aspects of meaning. For this reason, some classical scholars lament the modernized translations of Homer. One of them has argued that "the translator has to aim not at assimilating 'otherness' into English, but in moving English into some kind of 'otherness.' He has to let his own language be powerfully affected by another one."[5]

[3] M. F. Wiles, "Origen as Biblical Scholar," *CHB* 1:454–89, esp. p. 488.

[4] To make matters worse, it is not even clear how a "literal translation" can be identified. See in particular James Barr, *Typology of Literalism in Ancient Biblical Translations* (MSU 15; Göttingen: Vandenhoeck & Ruprecht, 1979). For a more recent attempt to clarify the issues, see E. Tov and B. G. Wright, "Computer-Assisted Study of the Criteria for Assessing the Literalness of Translation Units in the LXX," *Textus* 12 (1985): 149–87.

[5] William Arrowsmith, professor of classics at Johns Hopkins University, as reported in *Chronicle of Higher Education* 20:4 (March 1980): 1. Soon after the

The view that a translation ought to preserve not only the content but also the form of the original has the support of a few modern and knowledgeable writers. Perhaps the most striking example is Hölderlin, the nineteenth-century German poet who attempted to translate, in a most literal way, several difficult Greek writers, including Pindar. The results appear bizarre, but the project had a carefully defined logic and cannot be simply dismissed as irrational. Indeed, as highly respected a figure as George Steiner argues eloquently for the validity of this approach:

> Charged as it is with stylistic genius and interpretative audacity, Hölderlin's art of translation always derives from literalism, almost, in fact, from a literalism not only of the single word but of the letter. . . . Paradoxically, therefore, the most exalted vision we know of the nature of translation derives precisely from the programme of literalism, of word-for-word meta-phrase which traditional theory has regarded as most puerile.[6]

I am not concerned at this point with evaluating the merits of the various approaches to biblical translation; another volume in the present series will consider that issue. For our purposes in this chapter we need only appreciate the fact that a literal method of interpretation, as exemplified in the translation of Aquila, is not merely the relic of a primitive era. One can find cultured, post-Enlightenment scholars, including a few who understand the contribution of modern general linguistics, who stand in the broad hermeneutical tradition to which Aquila belongs.

If these facts appear disconcerting, note that we can also draw surprising parallels at the other end of the hermeneutical spectrum, namely, with respect to the allegorical approach associated with Origen's work (see below, pp. 56–57). It may

---

complete NEB was released, I heard a radio program in England devoted to its evaluation. Some literary critics strongly objected to the way this new version avoided literal translations of transparent Hebrew idioms in the Psalms. Not only did this approach insult the intelligence of modern readers, they claimed, but it also reduced Hebrew poetry to banality.

[6]George Steiner, *After Babel: Aspects of Language and Translation* (London: Oxford University Press, 1975), pp. 322–33, esp. p. 333.

be useful to point out, incidentally, that the opposition between these two approaches is only apparent, since "literal" and "figurative" often operate at different conceptual levels.[7] Indeed, one can say that these two methods achieve the same end: getting "behind" the text with a view to discovering meanings that are not obvious to the casual reader. For the moment, however, it will be useful to focus on the differences between the two methods and to keep in mind that, at least in the interpretation of numerous specific passages, they do in fact represent polar opposites.

THE PUZZLE OF HISTORICAL EXEGESIS

We would not be exaggerating greatly if we described the progress of biblical exegesis as the gradual abandonment of allegorical interpretation. One can point to some important moments in the history of the church that have aided this progress. As early as the fourth century, we find in Antiochene exegesis a fairly systematic program aimed at debunking the more objectionable features of Origen's approach. The twelfth-century intellectual renaissance saw, in the work of such writers as Peter the Chanter, significant shifts away from a predominant concern with the figurative sense of Scripture. And of greater importance in the theological arena was the attack on allegorical exegesis mounted by the Protestant Reformers.

Only after the eighteenth-century Enlightenment, however, did "scientific," grammatico-historical exegesis come into its own. By the time that Farrar wrote his *History of Interpretation* (1886), it was clear that the allegorical method had

---

[7] This factor may help to explain the apparent blurring of the distinctions from time to time. For example, we find it surprising to be told that "the great defect of medieval exegesis" was not so much its obsession with allegory but "an excess of literalism, or even more, an excess of historicism" (Don Jean Leclercq, "From Gregory the Great to St. Bernard," *CHB* 2:195). Perhaps related to this question is the argument by N. R. M. de Lange, *Origen and the Jews: Studies in Jewish-Christian Relations in Third Century Palestine* (Cambridge: Cambridge University Press, 1976), p. 110, that one can detect similarities between Origen and Akiba.

completely lost respectability in the scholarly establishment. One could no longer expect such a method to shed any light on the meaning of the text. One now had to pay exclusive attention to the text's historical meaning, that is, the meaning intended by the biblical author.

This description, however, leaves out a series of interesting and suggestive bits of information. It is simplistic, for example, to view Origen and the Antiochenes as representing two opposite approaches more or less exclusive of each other.[8] As we shall see, Origen used and defended literal interpretation on a number of occasions. Moreover, certain exegetical features that we would quickly dismiss as in some sense "allegorical" were consciously adopted as legitimate by the Antiochene exegetes. A striking example is one of John Chrysostom's homilies on the Gospel of John. Dealing with the wedding at Cana, he comments:

> At that time, therefore, Jesus made wine from water, and both then and now He does not cease changing wills that are weak and inconstant. There are men who are no different from water: cold and weak and inconstant. Accordingly, let us bring to the Lord those who are thus disposed, so as to cause their will to change and become like wine, so that it no longer is inconstant, but steadfast, and they become a cause of rejoicing both for themselves and for others.[9]

And Theodoret, whose historical commentaries are highly regarded, has this to say about Isaac's reference to the dew from heaven and the fatness of the earth (Gen. 27:39):

---

[8]Perhaps the clearest and most helpful brief comparison between the Alexandrian and Antiochene schools is to be found in chap. 2 of D. S. Wallace-Hadrill, *Christian Antioch: A Study of Early Christian Thought in the East* (Cambridge: Cambridge University Press, 1982). Pp. 33–35 show the high degree of variability among the Antiochenes themselves; Theodore of Mopsuestia was the most extreme in emphasizing historical exegesis.

[9]John Chrysostom, *Commentary on Saint John the Apostle and Evangelist: Homilies 1–47*, trans. T. A. Goggin (Fathers of the Church 33; Washington, D.C.: Catholic University of America Press, 1957), p. 219. Note also on p. 310 the ending of his otherwise very historical explanation of John 4:1–12.

These things according to the obvious superficial sense of the letter denote grace from above and abundance of blessings from the earth; but according to the higher interpretation they depict the *divinity* of the Lord Christ by means of the expression *dew*; and by the fatness of the earth, his *humanity* received from us.[10]

We are also puzzled to find that, in the Middle Ages, a renewed appreciation for the *sensus literalis* did not mean an abandonment of allegorical exegesis. Modern students find it difficult to develop sympathy for the intellectual work of medieval scholars, partly because one can easily find examples of overly subtle or trivial reasoning that appears to discredit scholastic thinking.

We have all had our laughs hearing about the serious attention paid by Schoolmen to such questions as whether men at the resurrection will recover all the fingernail clippings they lost during their lives, whether several angels can simultaneously occupy the same physical space, and so on. A good case can be made, however, for the thesis that the development of the scientific method was directly dependent on the kinds of debates refined during the scholastic period.[11]

More relevant for us is the recent work on medieval exegesis. We now realize, for example, that Hugh of St. Victor, by carefully differentiating the literal sense from the allegorical and the tropological, "enormously increased the dignity of the historical sense. . . . The importance of the letter is constantly stressed."[12]

---

[10]Quoted in Davidson, *Sacred Hermeneutics,* p. 143. Even Theodore of Mopsuestia, for all his relentless attack on allegorical interpretation, occasionally allowed himself some freedom, as in his exposition of Psalm 45. See Dimitri Z. Zaharopoulos, "Theodore of Mopsuestia's Critical Methods in Old Testament Study" (Ph.D. diss., Boston University, 1964), pp. 192–93; see pp. 228–30 for Theodore's views on prophecy.

[11]Christopher Dawson, *Religion and the Rise of Western Culture* (Garden City, N.Y.: Doubleday, 1958; orig. 1950), pp. 17–22, 189–91.

[12]Smalley, *Study of the Bible,* p. 89; cf. also the quotations she gives on subsequent pages. Hugh's disciple, Andrew, went as far as to interpret Isaiah 53 without reference to Christ (p. 185). A good sampling of Hugh's work may be found in James J. Megivern, *Official Catholic Teachings: Biblical Interpretation* (Wilmington, N.C.: McGrath, 1978), pp. 161–66.

Such a notable flourishing of grammatical exegesis meant that many Schoolmen could no longer be satisfied with the effort to resolve contradictions by appealing to allegorical meaning. "Sometimes the contradiction appears to lie between two literal meanings. It was above all in dealing with such cases that the twelfth century interpreters made their new contribution" by paying careful attention to the nature of language, lexical usage, rhetorical questions, and so on.[13]

This concern for historical exegesis, however, did not suspend the need for allegorical interpretation. And the resulting tension is seen most clearly in the work of Rupert of Deutz (d. ca. 1129), for whom

> the letter gives instruction in holiness, but the mystical sense is a demonstration or prophecy of something far higher. Everywhere in Rupert's exegesis we can feel his consciousness of this lively tension between the literal and the spiritual senses, as he looks for the "incorporeal and invisible" which is to come and which is foreshadowed by the "corporeal and visible" deeds done in the past. The literal sense is a veil over the beauties which Grace reveals, and which a man must search for in the mirror of his sense-impressions.[14]

Although one might think otherwise, the Reformation did not fully resolve the basic tension. The view that the Protestant Reformers broke with the allegorical method and argued passionately for the *sensus literalis* is of course accurate. It is also accurate to point out that John Calvin in particular translated this concern into practice. Calvin's commentaries are an extraordinary testimony to sober, historical exegesis at a time when the dominant approach was motivated by other concerns.[15]

---

[13] G. R. Evans, *The Language and Logic of the Bible: The Earlier Middle Ages* (Cambridge: Cambridge University Press, 1984), p. 143. See especially her discussion of Peter the Chanter (pp. 146–63).

[14] Ibid., p. 15.

[15] See Hans-Joachim Kraus, "Calvin's Exegetical Principles," *Int* 31 (1977): 8–18, esp. the principle of lucid brevity, p. 12. For greater detail, Richard C. Gamble, "*Brevitas et facilitas:* Toward an Understanding of Calvin's Hermeneutic," *WTJ* 47 (1985): 1–17. Calvin, incidentally, thought very highly of

On the other hand, the challenge of figurative exegesis did not go away. Luther, for example, was somewhat inconsistent in the application of his principle; moreover, he acknowledged, on the basis of Galatians 4:21–31, that allegories may be used as pretty ornaments.[16] Calvin is more consistent in his use of the grammatico-historical method (see his commentary on Gal. 4:22), yet at one point he remarks that God's promise to Abraham, according to Paul, "is to be fulfilled, *not only allegorically* but literally, for Abraham's physical offspring."[17] And as is well known, differences among the Reformers concerning figurative language in the Bible came to a head in the debates regarding the significance of the Lord's Supper.[18]

But the greatest puzzle of all is that twentieth-century scholars have raised anew the question whether we need to be bound in our interpretation by the historical intent of the biblical author! These modern scholars, to be sure, are not

---

Chrysostom and sought to emulate him. See John R. Walchenbach, "John Calvin as Biblical Commentator: An Investigation into Calvin's Use of John Chrysostom as an Exegetical Source" (Ph.D. diss., University of Pittsburgh, 1974). More specialized is Alexandre Ganoczy and Klaus Müller, *Calvins handschriftliche Anotationen zu Chrysostomus: Ein Beitrag zur Hermeneutik Calvins* (Veröffentlichungen des Instituts für europäische Geschichte Mainz 102; Wiesbaden: F. Steiner, 1981); see pp. 28–31 on the question of literal meaning.

[16] See Farrar, *History,* p. 328. According to A. Skevington Wood, Luther recognized a Spirit-given sense as "a new interpretation, which is then the new literal sense" (*Luther's Principles of Biblical Interpretation* [London: Tyndale, 1960], p. 32). Wood considers that "in his recognition of a *sensus plenior* he was perhaps nearer to Origen then he knew."

[17] Calvin, *Institutes* 4. 16. 15 (p. 1337, my emphasis). In section 3. 4. 5 he rebuts a scholastic allegory of the raising of Lazarus by offering his own allegory. Although Calvin seems to propose this allegory partly tongue-in-cheek, the passage is suggestive. See also T. H. L. Parker, *Calvin's New Testament Commentaries* (Grand Rapids: Eerdmans, 1971). pp. 63–38, esp. p. 66.

[18] See J. Pelikan, *Reformation of Church and Dogma (1300–1700)* (The Christian Tradition 4; Chicago: University of Chicago Press, 1984), pp. 193–95. The seriousness of the problem is brought out by Roland H. Bainton, "The Bible in the Reformation," *CHB* 3.1–37, esp. pp. 29–30: with regard to the commandment against images, Carlstadt insisted on the literal meaning while Luther on the spiritual, yet the tables were completely reversed when they discussed the words "this is my body."

calling us back to practice Origenistic allegorizing, but the nature of the contemporary debate makes clear that we are not facing simple black-and-white choices.

Since contemporary figures are, strictly speaking, beyond the scope of a history of interpretation, we need not discuss them here. I mention only the work of Paul Ricoeur, a philosopher with broad interests who has paid special attention to the problems of biblical hermeneutics. His emphasis on what he calls the "reservoir of meaning" attached to all literary texts is by no means unique or extravagant.[19] Rather, it represents a more general reaction to certain literary theories (and to the common methods of biblical scholarship) that place primary or exclusive emphasis on historical interpretation. The question "What did the author mean?" is now regarded as still valid but largely uninteresting. The literary text, we are told, lives on long after its author is dead, and so the ideas that later readers associate with that text can and must be viewed as part of its meaning.

The point of view just described is the source of considerable debate, but broad segments of modern scholarship regard it as plausible and even respectable. What needs to be noted here is that biblical scholarship, after triumphantly demonstrating that grammatico-historical exegesis is all that really matters, is being pressed on various sides to acknowledge that maybe there is something "behind" or "around" the text (at any rate, distinct from the original author's intent) that should be regarded as part of its meaning. And for all the significant differences between an Origen and a Ricoeur, it is precisely this feature that was earlier thought to be completely unacceptable in the allegorical method.

---

[19] See Paul Ricoeur, *Essays on Biblical Interpretation* (Philadelphia: Fortress, 1980), esp. pp. 49–57 for his discussion of allegorical and similar approaches. Note also David C. Steinmetz, "The Superiority of Pre-Critical Exegesis," *Ex Auditi* 1 (1985): 74–82 (orig. in *Theology Today* 37 [1980]: 27–38), esp. p. 82: "The medieval theory of levels of meaning in the biblical text, with all its undoubted defects, flourished because it is true, while the modern theory of a single meaning, with all its demonstrable virtues, is false."

UNDERSTANDING ORIGEN

We find, then, a curious ambiguity throughout the history of literal interpretation. Origen can hardly be blamed for this state of affairs—he simply managed to pose the hermeneutical problem in a particularly forceful way. Perhaps he can also help us to find a way to its solution.

For Origen, literal meanings are indeed important. In his most basic theological work, *On First Principles,* he stresses the fact that most of the narrative material in Scripture is historical. Somewhat condescendingly, it is true, Origen explains that the literal meaning is useful for simple believers, the implication being that truly mature Christians will be able to see beyond the literal.[20]

But other passages make it plain that he sincerely viewed the literal meaning as important. Origen's interpretation of Psalm 37, for example, "is presented as exegesis of the original historical sense, and not as exegesis of another and higher content behind the historical. The allegorical meaning is itself to be found within the historical sense of the text."[21] Again, when he addresses an accusation by Celsus that the story of Lot and his two daughters in Genesis 19 is iniquitous, Origen criticizes Celsus for not paying attention to the ordinary sense of the passage. Indeed, Origen regards it as a mark of the Bible's superiority over pagan writers that the literal meaning of Scripture is morally commendable.[22]

As one begins to appreciate the character of Origen's debate with Celsus, a remarkable fact emerges. Among the Greeks, divine inspiration and allegorical meaning were often seen as coordinate, especially in the case of Homer. As a result,

---

[20] Origen, *On First Principles* 4. 3. 4; 4. 2. 5 (pp. 294–96, 278).

[21] Karen Jo Torjesen, *Hermeneutical Procedure and Theological Method in Origen's Exegesis* (PTS 28; Berlin: W. de Gruyter, 1986), p. 23.

[22] Origen, *Contra Celsum* 4. 45 and 1. 17–18 (*ANF* 4:518 and 403), referred to by Dan G. McCartney, "Literal and Allegorical Interpretation in Origen's *Contra Celsum,*" *WTJ* 48 (1986): 281–301, esp. pp. 288–89. For other examples, see R. P. C. Hanson, *Allegory and Event: A Study of the Sources and Significance of Origen's Interpretation of Scripture* (London: SCM, 1959), p. 238. Note also Wiles, "Origen," pp. 470–74.

Origen was obliged to formulate his views of biblical interpretation in response to two quite different lines of attack. On the one hand, some people objected that Christians resorted to strained allegorizing to save themselves from embarrassment. On the other hand, an inability to interpret the Bible allegorically might be understood as evidence that the Bible was not inspired.

It is fascinating, therefore, to see Origen downplaying allegorical interpretation by asserting the truth, goodness, and value of the Bible's literal meaning (over against pagan myths, which can *only* be interpreted allegorically). At the same time, Origen devotes much of books 4 and 5 in *Contra Celsum* justifying the allegorical method; after all, the skill of allegorical interpretation is regarded by both Celsus and Origen as a sign of intelligence.[23]

We would be quite wrong, however, to think that Origen defended the allegorical method simply to win points with his intellectual contemporaries. Quite the contrary, he viewed the method as having basic theological significance. In the first place, he argued that the unbelief of the Jews could be traced to their insistence that the prophecies be interpreted literally.[24] We may want to respond, of course, that the application of the Old Testament prophecies to Christ is something quite different from allegorical interpretation. But it is important for us to understand that Origen himself did not see a substantial difference between the two approaches.

The question whether Old Testament prophecies should be interpreted literally is a fascinating problem that has surfaced repeatedly throughout church history. In the Middle Ages, for example, scholars devoted considerable attention to the precise classification of the various senses of Scripture, and messianic prophecies created a special difficulty.

The Jews had been accused of interpreting Scripture "according to the letter", instead of according to the life-giving spirit. Was their interpretation of Old Testament prophecy to be called "the

---

[23] McCartney, "Literal and Allegorical," pp. 292–93.
[24] Origen, *On First Principles* 4. 2. 1, p. 270.

literal sense" of the prophecy, while the christological interpretation went under the heading "spiritual or allegorical"? This division seemed to clash with the received teaching that the literal sense was true and basic.[25]

Moreover, we should appreciate the substantive parallel between Origen's controversy with the Jews and modern debates touching on whether the Old Testament prophecies regarding the future of Israel will be interpreted literally. In one of the most popular premillennialist books at the turn of the last century, the story is told of a Jew who asked a Christian minister whether he took literally Gabriel's promise that Mary's son would reign over Jacob (Luke 1:32–33). The minister responded that the prophecy referred to Christ's spiritual reign over the church, to which the Jew replied: "Then . . . neither do I believe literally the words preceding, which say that this Son of David should be born of a virgin; but take them to be merely a figurative manner of describing the remarkable character for purity of him who is the subject of the prophecy."[26]

Second, Origen was convinced that to interpret everything literally would necessarily lead to blasphemy or contradiction. This sentiment has been shared by many other believers.[27] Particularly significant is the experience of Augustine, who for a time struggled with what he felt were offensive elements in the Old Testament. Finally, he heard with delight Ambrose's emphasis on 2 Corinthians 3:6 ("the letter kills, but the Spirit gives life"): "drawing aside the mystic veil, he spiritually laid

[25] Beryl Smalley, "The Bible in the Medieval Schools," *CHB* 2:197–220, esp. p. 214. Cf. also Erwin I. J. Rosenthal, "The Study of the Bible in Medieval Judaism," ibid., pp. 252–79, esp. pp. 256, 268. Esra Shereshevsky's wonderful book *Rashi: The Man and His World* (New York: Sepher-Hermon, 1982) devotes chap. 5 to this general question.

[26] W. E. Blackstone, *Jesus Is Coming* (New York: Revell, 1898), pp. 20–21.

[27] On Jerome, see H. F. D. Sparks, "Jerome as Biblical Scholar," *CHB* 1:510–41, esp. p. 538: "To take some passages in the Old Testament literally would be either absurd or unedifying: Hosea cannot possibly be taken literally (for 'God commands nothing except what is honourable'); while to interpret Revelation literally would be to reduce it to the level of a purely Jewish tract." Similarly, the Reformed theologian Francis Turretin, *The Doctrine of Scripture*, trans. J. W. Beardslee III (Grand Rapids: Baker, 1981), p. 208.

open that which, accepted to the 'letter,' seemed to teach perverse doctrines."[28]

Here again, Origen and most ancients apparently failed to appreciate that what we may call a "straightforward" reading of the text—that is, one that is sensitive to simple figures of speech used by the biblical author—is more than adequate to avoid the problems he feared.[29] In some respects, however, the difference between Origen and many modern interpreters is often one of degree, that is, of where the line is drawn between figurative and nonfigurative interpretation. There is little if any substantive difference, for example, between the way that Origen or a modern scholar would argue that the Bible uses anthropomorphisms to speak of God.

Third, Origen was convinced that the New Testament itself, by using allegory, establishes the validity of the method. In this connection he can appeal to 1 Corinthians 9:9–10; 10:1–4; Galatians 4:21–31; and even Ephesians 5:31–32.[30] In particular, his homilies on Exodus (section 5. 1) deal with Paul's use of the Old Testament narrative in 1 Corinthians 10:

---

[28] Augustine, *Confessions* 6. 4 (*NPNF*, 1st ser., 1:92). See also *On Christian Doctrine* 3. 5 (*NPNF* 2:559). Among many works devoted to Augustine's views, see Charles J. Costello, *St. Augustine's Doctrine on the Inspiration and Canonicity of Scripture* (Washington, D.C.: Catholic University of America, 1930), pp. 45–56, which focus on the issue of historicity. Gerhard Strauss, *Schriftgebrauch, Schriftauslegung, und Schriftbeweis bei Augustin* (BGBH 1; Tübingen: J. C. B. Mohr, 1959), esp. chaps. 3–4, which amount to a (difficult) commentary on *On Christian Doctrine*. Clearer and more comprehensive is Belford D. Jackson, "Semantics and Hermeneutics in Saint Augustine's *De doctrina Christiana*" (Ph.D. diss., Yale University, 1967), esp. pp. 171–87, which emphasize Augustine's theory of signs. More recently, Bertrand de Margerie has devoted volume 3 of *Introduction à l'histoire de l'exégèse* (Paris: Cerf: 1980–83) to Augustine; note pp. 98–100, which bring Ricoeur into the picture.

[29] Perhaps only Theodore of Mopsuestia clearly and explicitly included metaphorical meaning as part of the literal meaning. See Alexander Kerrigan, *St. Cyril of Alexandria: Interpreter of the Old Testament* (AnBib 2; Rome: Pontificio Istituto Biblico, 1952), pp. 51–56; note also p. 58 on Jerome and p. 86 on Cyril.

[30] See Origen, *Contra Celsum* 4. 49 (*ANF* 4:520) and *On First Principles* 4. 2. 6, p. 280.

> You observe how greatly the sense Paul gives us differs from the
> narrative of the text. . . . Does it not seem right to keep a rule of
> this kind, as given to us, by observing a like standard in other
> cases? or, as some desire, are we to desert what the great and
> noble Apostle has told us and turn again to Jewish fables?[31]

His use of these passages makes it plain that one of our main
difficulties is that of definition. We must return to the question
of choosing the criteria that help us to establish what counts as
allegorical interpretation.

Fourth, Origen stresses that part of the divine aim is to
veil the truth. Origen is not as emphatic on this point as his
predecessor Clement of Alexandria, but he does bring it up in
some important passages.[32] At the very beginning of *On First
Principles,* he states that the whole church believes that there is a
secret meaning in the Bible that is hidden from the majority.
Obviously this comment raises the larger question whether the
Bible ought to be regarded as clear or obscure, the topic of
chapter 4.

One aspect of this question, however, requires discussion
here, and we may view it as a fifth point, namely, Origen's
conception of human weaknesses in spiritual understanding. For
Origen himself, this consideration afforded a means of distinguishing between immature and mature believers: the latter,
through their skill in allegorical interpretation, show that they
have the key to knowledge.[33] Whether consciously or not,
Origen tends therefore to identify spiritual maturity with
intellectual prowess.

On the other hand, once we relate human weakness to the
allegorical method, a more positive development of the concept

---

[31] Quoted in R. B. Tollinton, *Selections from the Commentaries and Homilies of
Origen* (London: SPCK, 1929), pp. 72–74.

[32] Origen, *On First Principles* 4. 2. 8; 4. 3. 1, 11 (pp. 284, 288, 305). From a
different perspective, note Augustine's remark: "Some of the expressions are so
obscure as to shroud the meaning in the thickest darkness. And I do not doubt
that all this was *divinely arranged* for the purpose of subduing pride by toil and of
preventing a feeling of satiety in the intellect, which generally holds in small
esteem what is discovered without difficulty" (*On Christian Doctrine* 2. 6. 7,
quoted by Gerald Bonner, "Augustine as Biblical Scholar," *CHB* 1:547).

[33] Origen, *On First Principles* 4. 1. 7; 4. 2. 3 (pp. 267–68, 274–75).

becomes possible. Indeed, "the whole of medieval exegesis is founded" on the assumption that we can understand God only dimly and that therefore he adapts his word to our damaged mental faculty.[34] An important exponent of this concept was Gregory the Great, whose writings played a foundational role in the development of medieval theology. In his view, those embarrassing features of the Bible that appear like banalities should be understood as evidences of God's mercy, for they show his willingness to speak in a way we can understand.

What appears strange, defective, or false is not really a fault in Scripture, but one in us. Paradoxically, biblical difficulties become aids for us. "Each obscure or tortuous narrative, each ambiguity or contradiction, meets an obscurity or twist or confusion in human thinking and is thus more, not less, intelligible to man's clouded sinful mind.[35]

ALLEGORY AND PRACTICAL APPLICATION

It should be clear by now that the allegorical method was not an isolated quirk among early Christians. They did not adopt it arbitrarily or unthinkingly but viewed it rather as one of the foundation stones in a large theological and intellectual edifice.

But there is more to say about the method. Quite apart from broad theological commitments, allegorical interpretations are very difficult to avoid for a believer who wishes to apply the truth of Scripture to his or her life. One already senses this concern in the writings of Philo, who argued that there was no real point in reading about Abraham's journeys unless they refer to spiritual journeys in which we too participate.[36]

---

[34] Evans, *Language and Logic,* p. 1.

[35] Ibid., p. 3. See also Evans's work *The Thought of Gregory the Great* (Cambridge: Cambridge University Press, 1986), p. 95.

[36] Samuel Sandmel, *Philo of Alexandria: An Introduction* (New York: Oxford University Press, 1979), p. 25. On Philo's exegesis, see the important contribution by B. L. Mack, "Philo Judaeus and Exegetical Traditions in Alexandria," *ANRW* 2. 25. 2, pp. 227–71. For greater detail, see Irmgard Christiansen, *Die Technik der allegorischen Auslegungswissenschaft bei Philon von*

Similarly, Origen believed that the spiritual sense contains universal significance and shows "how the hearer or reader participates in" the history of salvation. Indeed, "For Origen it is most of all the 'usefulness' . . . of Scripture which inspiration through the Holy Spirit guarantees."[37]

But Origen was hardly peculiar in this respect. The purpose of all the Fathers in studying Scripture was "purely practical, and we do not understand their exegesis until we understand this."[38] Augustine himself provides a good illustration. In *On Christian Doctrine* 3. 10 (*NPNF* 2:560), after he has condemned interpretations that take literally that which is figurative ("a miserable slavery"), he also warns of taking the literal in a figurative way. How, then, does one differentiate between the two? "And the way is certainly as follows: Whatever then is in the word of God that cannot, when taken literally, be referred either to purity of life or soundness of doctrine, you may set down as figurative." As this subsequent discussion makes clear, Augustine has in mind here the command to love God and neighbor. This practical concern has

---

Alexandrien (BGBH 7; Tübingen: J. C. B. Mohr, 1969). Several essays on biblical interpretation are included in Yehoshua Amir, *Die hellenistische Gestalt des Judentums bei Philon von Alexandrien* (Forschungen zum jüdisch-christlichen Dialog 5; Neukirchen-Vluyn: Neukirchener, 1983); note esp. "Rabbinischer Midrasch und philonische Allegorese," pp. 107–18.

[37] Torjesen, *Hermeneutical Procedure*, pp. 68–69, 124. On p. 126, Torjesen points out that this usefulness of Scripture is inherent in the meaning of the text; therefore, a distinction must be made between Origen's view and the modern understanding about application. On pp. 25–26, she remarks that, since Origen is intensely interested in the situation of the hearer, his exegesis of the original situation of the psalmist already includes its significance for the hearer, so that in this case there is no need for a separate task of allegorical exegesis. On the general question, note Jaroslav Pelikan, *The Emergence of the Catholic Tradition (100–600)* (The Christian Tradition 1; Chicago: University of Chicago Press, 1971), pp. 60–62. A negative aspect is pointed out by Hanson: while Origen's exegesis of Jeremiah 13:12 is admirable in many respects, "his interpretation is vitiated by his reliance on a faulty translation and his determination to extort some immediately edifying meaning from the passage" (*Allegory*, p. 179).

[38] R. P. C. Hanson, "Biblical Exegesis in the Early Church," *CHB* 1:412–53.

become for him a basic hermeneutical principle that allows allegorizing.[39]

Medieval scholars were no different. Smalley asks why the historical approach of the Antiochenes was neglected in the Middle Ages. "The answer must be that our Latin student preferred the Alexandrian method to the Antiochene. The former satisfied a paramount emotional need and corresponded to a world outlook while the latter struck him as cold and irrelevant."[40] Indeed, they might well have put it this way: "What value is there in the Bible if all you can do is state what the text says?" In the mind of the Schoolmen, there was no significant difference between applying the text and allegorizing. And we need to admit that *in practice* there is often very little difference.

Perhaps two modern examples will shed light on this problem. C. S. Lewis was a twentieth-century believer, far removed in time and culture from the likes of Origen. Moreover, Lewis was not a backwoods Fundamentalist but a highly respected literary scholar. Toward the end of his popular little book *Reflections on the Psalms,* Lewis addresses the perplexing problem of the imprecatory psalms. Here is his personal solution to that problem:

> Of the cursing Psalms I suppose most of us make our own moral allegories. . . . We know the proper object of utter hostility— wickedness, especially our own. From this point of view I can use even the horrible passage in [Psalm] 137 about dashing the Babylonian babies against the stones. I know things in the inner world which are like babies; the infantile beginnings of small indulgences, small resentments, which may one day become dipsomania or settled hatred, but which woo us and wheedle us with special pleadings and seem so tiny, so helpless that in resisting them we feel we are being cruel to animals. They begin whimpering to us "I don't ask much, but", or "I had at least hoped", or "you owe yourself *some* consideration". Against all such pretty infants (the dears have such winning ways) the advice

[39] See Jackson, "Semantics," pp. 79–86, and Preus, *Shadow*, p. 13.
[40] Smalley, *Study of the Bible*, p. 19.

of the Psalm is the best. Knock the little bastards' brains out. And "blessed" is he who can, for it's easier said than done.[41]

My other example is a contemporary preacher I know who combines in a marvelous way theological soundness, academic achievement, and eloquence. Not too long ago I heard him preach a superb sermon on the raising of Lazarus. He had obviously done his exegetical homework, and up to the last five or ten minutes, he kept close to his text and communicated to the congregation, clearly and vigorously, the theological significance of John 11. In his church, however, there is great emphasis on the need to be practical and to apply the text as explicitly as possible to the audience, most of whom are believers. As he addressed the question "What does this mean to you?" he began to relate the raising of Lazarus to the believer's sanctification. There is of course nothing theologically wrong with viewing resurrection as a picture of sanctification (see Rom. 6:1–4). It seems fairly clear, however, that the idea was far removed from John's mind as he penned the eleventh chapter of his gospel. This preacher was therefore obligated to use the text allegorically, stating that, when Jesus orders that the grave clothes be removed from Lazarus, he is ordering us to remove the sins from our lives.[42]

It is unnecessary to point out that every hour of every day thousands of Christians allegorize the Scriptures as they seek to find spiritual guidance. Moreover, many of the most effective preachers the Christian church has seen made consistent use of this approach. Charles Spurgeon, the nineteenth-century Bap-

---

[41] C. S. Lewis, *Reflections on the Psalms* (New York: Harcourt Brace Jovanovich, 1958), p. 136.

[42] Interestingly, Frei views application as something like an extension of typology, which is figural interpretation (*Eclipse,* p. 3). If a preacher is very concerned about direct application but does not wish to resort to allegorizing, the result is often a different sermon altogether, as happens not infrequently in Puritan works and quite characteristically in Chrysostom's homilies, "which show a sharp break in continuity as Chrysostom moves on from exegesis to the pressing issues of contemporary society—a difficulty faced by every preacher who roots himself firmly in sober, historical exegesis" (M. F. Wiles, "Theodore of Mopsuestia as Representative of the Antiochene School," *CHB* 1:490).

tist preacher whose powerful sermons exerted a tremendous
influence week by week throughout the Christian world, is one
of the clearest examples.

None of this makes the method right, and it certainly
would be wrong-headed to suggest that allegorical interpretation be rehabilitated in modern scholarship. On the other hand,
we can hardly justify developing a hermeneutical approach that
works in splendid isolation from the way believers usually read
the Scriptures. And the force of this consideration is pressed
upon us when we realize that the method played a significant
role in the shaping of Christian theology.[43]

Without attempting in our brief space to solve this
difficult problem, we may take note of two or three relevant
points. In the first place, the allegorical or "free" use of
Scripture has much in common with the way literature in
general is often handled. Numerous public speakers, especially
if they are well read, will pepper their discourses with allusions
to literary themes or actual quotations, even though the original
context had little or nothing to do with the contemporary
concerns to which they are being applied. In other words, there
is a stylistic or emotional force about such a use of literature that
appears to justify it (at least one never hears objections to this
practice, so long as it does not show up in a proper commentary
on the works themselves).

Similarly, we all know ministers who, when preaching on
a particular topic, will ignore passages that address that topic
directly and choose for their text a passage that does not.
Certainly it is much more exciting for the congregation to hear
an eloquent sermon on a passage that they had no idea meant
what the preacher is taking it to mean than to listen through a
careful exposition of what a passage plainly says!

In short, much allegorical exposition arises from the need
for rhetorical effect. Unfortunately, to the extent that the

---

[43]For a particularly interesting example, see Jaroslav Pelikan, "The 'Spiritual
Sense' of Scripture: The Exegetical Basis for St. Basil's Doctrine of the Holy
Spirit," in *Basil of Caesarea: Christian, Humanist, Ascetic. A Sixteen-Hundredth
Anniversary Symposium*, 2 vols. ed. P. J. Fedwick (Toronto: Pontifical Institute
of Medieval Studies, 1981) 1:337–60.

congregation learns thereby to look for "hidden meanings" in the text, to that extent the text is either subjected to greater distortions or else it is removed from the common believer who is unable to produce exegetical surprises.

In the second place, allegorizing is difficult to resist because the believer, quite naturally, expects the Word of God to say and do more than is immediately apparent. Clearly, it is not simply the literary power of allegory that appeals to a Christian congregation. Our commitment to the divine inspiration of Scripture raises certain expectations in our minds as to what we are likely to find in it.

This approach to Scripture is especially prominent in the Pietist tradition. The eighteenth-century theologian J. J. Rambach, for example, stressed the Spirit's work both in the inspiration of Scripture and in the believer's reading. This view, as Frei puts it,

> demands that one be able to discern a spiritual sense above the ordinary grammatical and logical senses in at least some of the sacred words. Moreover, the spiritual sense of such individual words lends them an expanded force or emphasis, so that they have as much meaning and resonance attributed to them as they can possibly bear. "Emphasis" becomes a technical term. It stands for a doctrine or a way of seeing a meaning of scriptural words quite beyond what they appear to have in ordinary usage or in their immediate context.[44]

In a very important sense, we are quite right to assume that there is more to a passage than its obvious meaning, for our conception of the unity of the Bible requires us to assess specific portions in the light of the whole tenor of Scripture. We could argue, for example, that, when a preacher sees the doctrine of Christian sanctification taught in John 11, he is merely exploiting certain associations that are made explicit elsewhere.

It would be better, of course, if the minister makes clear that the passage in question does not address sanctification directly, but there is nothing inherently wrong in his reminding the congregation that the Scriptures do in fact use the figure of

---

[44]Frei, *Eclipse*, p. 38.

resurrection to shed light on the doctrine of sanctification. Interestingly, Origen himself justified the use of allegory on the grounds that he was concerned to grasp the *entire* meaning of the biblical material.[45] This matter will come up again in chapter 4.

Wallace-Hadrill provides a marvelous illustration of the way in which cross-fertilization between passages can take place on the basis of belief in the unity of Scripture. Psalm 110:7 says, "He will drink from a brook beside the way; therefore he will lift up his head." Eusebius finds that, by referring to Psalm 123:4, he can link together the two Psalm references with Matthew 26:4; Philippians 2:8; and Ephesians 1:20. On the basis of Psalm 123:4, "the brook" must mean

> the time of temptations: *our soul hath passed through the brook, yea, our soul hath passed through the deep waters.* He therefore drinks in the brook, it says, that cup evidently of which He darkly spoke at the time of His passion, when He said: *Father, if it be possible let this cup pass from Me.* . . . It was, then, by drinking this cup that He lifted up His head, as the apostle also says, for when He was *obedient to the Father unto death, even the death of the Cross, therefore,* he says, *God hath highly exalted Him,* raising Him from the dead.[46]

TOWARD A DEFINITION OF ALLEGORY

I have so far used the term *allegory* rather loosely— deliberately so, since we need to appreciate fully the fact that, in the mind of Origen and many others, virtually any type of figurative interpretation could be described as allegorical. The terminological problem is a serious one, since even today the argument is sometimes heard that Paul believed in the allegorical method—after all, did he not use the term *allēgoreō* in Galatians 4:24? We can hardly assume, however, that the meaning we associate with the English term corresponds exactly with that of the cognate Greek verb. One could just as

---

[45] Origen, *On First Principles* 4. 3. 5, pp. 296–97.

[46] D. S. Wallace-Hadrill, *Eusebius of Caesarea* (London: A. R. Mowbray, 1960), p. 93.

easily argue, on the basis of the term *paroxysmos* in Acts 15:39, that Paul and Barnabas suffered physical convulsions over the question of whether Mark should accompany them.

A comparison between Paul's use of the Abraham-Hagar story in Galatians and Philo's allegorical treatment of that incident makes clear that the differences between the two approaches are much more significant than the similarities.[47] The fourth-century exegetes from Antioch appreciated the fact that, whatever else Paul intended by his reference to Genesis, he continued to affirm the narrative's historicity. In their attack upon Origen's allegorical method, therefore, they properly focused on Origen's tendency (not as pronounced as Philo's, to be sure) to downplay the historical character of Old Testament narratives.[48]

The Antiochenes themselves, of course, would not have denied the metaphorical character of many biblical passages. Moreover, they would have insisted that there is a higher, or spiritual, meaning (that is, a messianic reference) to the Old Testament prophecies. They used the term *theōria* to describe their position, a matter that will concern us again in chapter 5. Origen regarded such interpretations as instances of allegorizing, but the Antiochenes were correct in identifying the historical issue as a distinguishing feature that separated Paul's approach from Origen's. In their view, Paul was using *typology* in Galatians 4:21–31, that is, an interpretation that affirms the historicity of the narrative and then attempts to discover a theological significance in it; this deeper meaning, though perhaps not obvious on the face of the narrative, is closely tied to the literal meaning.[49]

---

[47] See J. B. Lightfoot, *The Epistle of St. Paul to the Galatians* (Grand Rapids: Zondervan, 1962; orig. 1865), pp. 198–200.

[48] See Hanson, *Allegory,* p. 52 and chap. 10. Critics of Origen have seldom been fair in failing to recognize Origen's relatively high regard for historicity, in contrast to Philo's customary approach.

[49] For a summary of the interpretations of Chrysostom, Theodore, and Theodoret, see Robert J. Kepple, "An Analysis of the Antiochene Exegesis of Galatians 4:24–26," *WTJ* 39 (1976–77): 239–49. Modern formulations have refined the concept of typology. One of the most helpful brief discussions is R. T. France, *Jesus and the Old Testament: His Application of Old Testament*

One can see why some scholars have objected to the distinction between allegory and typology. From one perspective one can argue that

> both allegory and *theōria* speak about the same anagogical dynamic Origen so eloquently described: the biblical text leads the reader upward into spiritual truths that are not immediately obvious and that provide a fuller understanding of God's economy of salvation. . . . The fact remains that in acknowledging the divine author of Scripture both sides sought deeper meaning and hidden treasures of revelation in the sacred text.[50]

We must admit that, as long as the allegorical method is perceived primarily as the attempt to look for a "deeper" or "higher" or "spiritual" meaning in the text, then the difference between it and typology seems trivial or even artificial. On the other hand, if we narrow the meaning of *allegorical* so that it describes a playing down or even a rejection of historicity, then the distinction becomes valid, useful, and important.

The qualification then needs to be made, however, that in this sense Origen himself did not adopt a full-blown allegorical approach. As we have seen, he sometimes defended the plain and historical meaning of narratives rather forcefully. Moreover, one may infer that he believed there should be a connection between such a meaning and the meanings arrived at

---

Passages to Himself and His Mission (Grand Rapids: Baker, 1982; orig. 1971), pp. 38–43.

[50] Karlfried Froehlich, trans. and ed., *Biblical Interpretation in the Early Church* (Sources of Early Christian Thought; Philadelphia: Fortress, 1984), pp. 20, 22. This volume includes an excellent translation of Theodore of Mopsuestia's commentary on Galatians 4:21–31, a basic source for our understanding of the controversy. The eighteenth-century skeptic Anthony Collins, incidentally, argued that "the meaningfulness of the biblical author's language must . . . be governed by the same criteria that govern the meaning of any proposition," yet this principle is "inapplicable to typological or allegorical or any other than literal meaning"; in short, nonliteral interpretation "results in rules that are completely arbitrary because they violate the natural use of language" (Frei, *Eclipse*, p. 82). For a more recent objection to the distinction between allegory and typology, see Paul K. Jewett, "Concerning the Allegorical Interpretation of Scripture," *WTJ* 17 (1954–55): 1–20.

through allegory (though we may wonder whether he really put this theory to practice with any consistency).

True, Origen denied the historicity of certain passages that, in his opinion, would be dishonoring to God if taken literally. In these cases, however, Origen would have probably argued that the biblical writers themselves did not intend the material to be taken literally.[51] We need to appreciate the fundamental difference between (1) the view that a biblical narrative, while intended as historical, should be more or less dehistoricized in favor of an allegorical interpretation, and (2) the view that the original point itself of a biblical passage is not historical.

Evangelicals recognize that the parables of Jesus, for example, are not necessarily historical but rather are fictional stories told for illustrative purposes. Many conservative scholars believe that the discourses in the Book of Job, whatever historical basis they may have, are not intended to be taken as transcriptions of what was said but represent a certain amount of creative stylization for purposes of dramatic effect.

In a recent and controversial commentary, the highly respected evangelical scholar R. H. Gundry has argued that Matthew wrote his gospel to present a semihistorical, drama-tized account of the life of Christ. One of many arguments Gundry used to support his position is that a literal, historical rendering of Matthew creates unbearable tensions between this gospel and the others—tensions that cannot be solved by a simple appeal to harmonization.

> Bending over backward for harmonizations results in falling flat on the ground. Furthermore, harmonizations often become so complicated that they are not only unbelievable, but also . . . damaging to the clarity of Scripture. They actually subvert

---

[51] Wiles comments: "How could the declared despiser of the 'letter' of scripture also hold that inspiration applied to every jot and tittle of the scriptural record? The answer lies in the fact that when Origen insists that every jot and tittle is inspired, he means every jot and tittle of the intended meaning. The minutest detail is important, but it is the detail spiritually understood that counts" ("Origen," p. 475).

scriptural authority by implicitly denying the plain meaning of the text.[52]

The parallels between this approach and Origen's are unmistakable. In both cases, we may want to respond that the narratives in question seem to present themselves as historical and that we would therefore need very compelling arguments to interpret them otherwise. I wish to point out, however, that the question of the allegorical method has not at all been raised in connection with Gundry's commentary; the reason is, of course, that Gundry has used a grammatico-historical approach to reach his conclusions. In a less obvious sense, however, Origen was following the same approach. He shows sensitivity to the importance of the author's intention, and that sensitivity we usually understand as the exact opposite of the allegorical method. In short, we cannot dismiss Origen's ideas on the grounds that he was merely allegorizing.

So much for the question of historicity. There are other ways, however, in which we may wish to restrict the meaning of *allegorical*. For example, for Philo the allegorical method was part of an involved *philosophical system*; similarly, there is a tendency in Origen's work to interpret biblical material as an expression of Christian Alexandrian philosophy. "The great value of allegory to those who practiced it was the way in which it made possible a theologically unified interpretation of the Bible as a whole."[53]

It would be self-delusion, however, to think that the absence of allegory guarantees protection against extrabiblical forms of thought. Theodore of Mopsuestia used the concept of historical development to unify biblical teaching. He introduced other concepts, however, not always consciously. "Like the allegorists, he may think that he has found the categories he needs from within scripture itself, when in fact he deceives himself in so thinking."[54]

A third aspect that helps us restrict the scope of what

[52]Gundry, *Matthew,* p. 626.
[53]Wiles, "Theodore of Mopsuestia," p. 508.
[54]Ibid., p. 509.

allegorical exegesis entails is that of *arbitrariness*. While doubtless neither Philo nor Origen would have accepted such a characterization of their approach, very frequently it is impossible to detect any necessary connection between the text and the meaning ascribed to it by Alexandrian allegorizers. Medieval scholars, to be sure, made a valiant effort to formulate guidelines and boundaries, but one cannot say that they succeeded. The most powerful argument against the allegorical method is that it seems to allow for no controls. In effect, anyone can see any meaning he or she wishes to see in any passage.[55]

Finally, we may define the method as requiring the presence of an *elite* group of interpreters—spiritual, mature believers who alone are given the key to the deeper meaning of Scripture. This feature of allegory is in some respects the most disagreeable one, and it leads very naturally into the subject of chapter 4.

But we must first summarize our findings. A rigorous definition of the allegorical method emphasizes its dehistoricizing, philosophizing, arbitrary, and elitist aspects. It is easy to prove that one can find no evidence of such a method in the New Testament. But we do an injustice to Origen and to most subsequent so-called allegorizers if we fail to note that they perceived their method as a broad approach to Scripture, one that was sensitive to the Bible's many figurative expressions, prophetic announcements, and suggestive associations. Note, for example, how Jeremiah 3:1 alludes to the law regarding divorce in Deuteronomy 24:1–4, but not in order to say anything about literal divorce. Rather the prophet uses it to

---

[55] Hanson reflects on the use of Proverbs 8:22 by various theologians in the early church: "It is indicative of the weakness of the exegetical principles adopted by the Fathers that these four writers, living in different times and in different places, could confidently quote exactly the same text in order to support four quite different Christological theories" ("Biblical Exegesis," p. 441). On p. 450, Hanson speaks of the method as "a technique for emancipating the exegete from bondage to the text." For a harsher (too harsh, I think) judgment of Origen's method, see Hanson, *Allegory*, pp. 245, 371. Note the discussion above concerning the Reformers' inconsistent use of literal versus figurative interpretation (p. 66).

introduce the Lord's judgment: "But you have lived as a prostitute with many lovers—would you now return to me?"[56]

Perhaps we can still learn from the great commentator J. B. Lightfoot, who can hardly be accused of using anything but the most sober grammatico-historical methods:

> The power of allegory has been differently felt in different ages, as it is differently felt at any one time by diverse nations. Analogy, allegory, metaphor—by what boundaries are these separated the one from the other? What is true or false, correct or incorrect, as an analogy or an allegory? What argumentative force must be assigned to either? We should at least be prepared with an answer to these questions, before we venture to sit in judgment on any individual case.[57]

Common believers routinely exploit these aspects, sometimes with damaging effects; they need to learn from professional exegetes how to develop historical and textual sensitivity. For their part, exegetes need to consider whether their work should reflect, to some extent, those qualities that believers give expression to when they read the Scriptures with little more than their faith. The answers are not easy to come by, but scholars and pastors can hardly afford to ignore the questions.

---

[56] See Fishbane, *Biblical Interpretation*, pp. 308–11.
[57] Lightfoot, *Galatians*, p. 200.

4

CLEAR OR OBSCURE?

REFORMATION DOCTRINE AND THE CONTEMPORARY CHALLENGE

It is no exaggeration to say that the sixteenth-century Reformation was, at bottom, a hermeneutical revolution. Luther's meeting with Cardinal Cajetan at Augsburg in 1518 developed into a discussion of *Unigenitus* (a papal bull published in 1343), which asserted the notion of a treasury of merits. In response Luther wrote a statement in which he refused "to discard so many important clear proofs of Scripture on account of a single ambiguous and obscure decretal of a Pope who is a mere human being." Not surprisingly, Cajetan objected that *someone* has to interpret the Bible and that the Pope is supreme in this area. Interpretation, however, had been a crucial element in Luther's "individual struggle for spiritual existence." He therefore unambiguously denied the Pope's supreme authority and proceeded to make his hermeneutical concerns a key element in the religious conflict that followed.[1]

The connection between this chapter and the previous one is very close. The main contribution of the Protestant Reformers to biblical hermeneutics is their insistence on *the plain*

---

[1] A. Skevington Wood, *Luther's Principles of Biblical Interpretation* (London: Tyndale, 1960), pp. 5–6.

meaning of Scripture. Their concern, however, focused specifically on the need to rescue the Bible from the allegorical method. We see this element strikingly expressed in many of Luther's remarks: "The Holy Spirit is the plainest writer and speaker in heaven and earth and therefore His words cannot have more than one, and that the very simplest sense, which we call the literal, ordinary, natural sense."[2] He can refer to allegories as dirt and scum that lead to idle speculations; indeed, for Luther, all heresies arise from neglecting the simple words of Scripture.[3]

As we have already noted, the contrast between the Reformers and the medieval scholastics should not be exaggerated. Not only had medieval scholarship made notable advances in historical and grammatical exegesis; it is also true that the Reformers' disapproval of allegory was not always consistent. Still, it is quite accurate to describe the Reformers as opponents of the allegorical method.

My concern in this chapter, however, is to identify their reason for that opposition. Up to the time of the Reformation, the Bible was perceived by most people as a fundamentally obscure book. The common folk could not be expected to understand it, and so they were discouraged from reading it.[4] Indeed the Bible was not even available in a language they could understand. They were almost completely dependent on the authoritative interpretation of the church.

But suppose the Bible is not to be allegorized. Suppose each passage has, not several meanings, but one, simple, literal meaning. In that case, all Christians may be encouraged to read

---

[2] *Works of Martin Luther* (Philadelphia: Holman, 1930) 3:350.

[3] Frederic W. Farrar, *History of Interpretation* (New York: Dutton, 1886), pp. 327–28.

[4] This statement is an overgeneralization and has been disputed, esp. by H. Rost, *Die Bibel im Mittelalter: Beiträge zur Geschichte und Bibliographie der Bibel* (Augsburg: Kommissions-Verlag M. Seitz, 1939). Moreover, Smalley points out that the revival of popular preaching in the twelfth century led to the use of allegory for the specific purpose of instructing the laity (*Study of the Bible*, p. 244). It can hardly be denied, however, that the authorities discouraged private Bible reading and that the problem became worse by the eve of the Reformation.

the Bible. The Scriptures should be translated into the common tongue. Each believer has a right to private interpretation. Luther in particular was very insistent on these points, and he expended tremendous energy on his most enduring work, the translation of the Bible into German.

The very fact that a *translation* was needed, however, raises certain problems for the view that the Scriptures are easily accessible to common Christians. If a Christian is unable to read the Bible in its original languages, then he or she is dependent on knowledgeable individuals to analyze the biblical text, understand its meaning, and express it clearly in the language of the reader. For this reason and others, many Christians feel that the doctrine of the clarity of Scripture has become more and more difficult to defend.

In the first place, the tremendous advances in specialized knowledge during the past century are sufficient to intimidate even the brashest among us. We could point to numerous interpretations of Scripture that have been proved wrong by recent advances. Does not that fact raise serious questions about the measure of certainty we can claim to have for our present opinions? What is true more generally seems also to be true of the interpretation of Scripture: the more we know, the more conscious we are of our ignorance.

In the second place, to say that the Scriptures are clear seems to fly in the face of the realities of contemporary church life. As pointed out in chapter 1, even those who share significant areas of doctrinal agreement find themselves at odds in the interpretation of important biblical passages—passages dealing with baptism and the Lord's Supper, passages that address the question of violence, and passages that have relevance for serious ethical problems such as war, capital punishment, and abortion. If those who are wholeheartedly devoted to the authority of Scripture cannot agree on such questions, has the doctrine of the clarity of Scripture become meaningless?

In the third place, there appears to be a new sensitivity to the significance of corporate authority in the church. The Reformers' emphasis on the right of private interpretation was often balanced by a recognition that no Christian is an island but is part of the body of Christ. Modern Evangelicalism, however, afraid of the abuse of church authority and influenced by a strong sense of individualism, has not always appreciated the need for Christians to submit their understanding of Scripture to the judgment of the established church.

Yet things seem to be changing. One detects a strong sense of humility among a growing number of believers. Without succumbing to the opposite danger of compromising their convictions, many Christians show a genuine desire to submit to the wisdom and counsel of their elders in the faith. Though this development is a wholesome one, does it not challenge our conviction that the meaning of the Scriptures is plain and readily accessible to the common reader?

ERASMUS VERSUS LUTHER

These questions are all serious, but they are not really new. Without minimizing the distinctive pressures that characterize modern Christianity, we need to appreciate how much help we can receive from Christians in earlier ages. Already in the fourth century, for example, John Chrysostom had recognized the need for both affirming and qualifying this notion of the clarity of Scripture: in his words, *panta ta anankaia dēla*, "all the things that are necessary are plain."[5] Even Origen, though not so explicitly, was making the same point when he argued that virtually all Christians understand what he believed to be one of the most fundamental doctrines: the spiritual significance of the law.[6]

A qualification of this sort may seem to leave the door open for abuse: could not someone define *necessary* and *fundamental* in such a way that vast portions of the Bible remain inaccessible to believers? Indeed one could, but we need to remember that such abuses are possible whenever we seek to be

---

[5] See Farrar, *History*, p. 329n. (I have not been able to verify Farrar's vague reference.)

[6] Origen, *On First Principles* 2. 7. 2, p. 117.

careful and responsible in our formulation of doctrine. Any attempt we make to avoid simplistic answers by clarifying and qualifying our statements runs the risk of being misunderstood and misapplied. It is important to note, however, that the Reformers themselves—tempted though they must have been to overstate their position in the face of controversy—defined their doctrine of biblical clarity, or perspicuity, by focusing on the foundational truths of Scripture.

Particularly instructive in this regard is Luther, since no one was more forceful in affirming that the meaning of the Bible is plain and accessible to all. Perhaps the most revealing discussion is found in his famous essay *On the Bondage of the Will,* in which he responded to a series of criticisms Erasmus had made some time earlier.[7] Erasmus, in the preface to his work *On the Freedom of the Will,* had objected to Luther's statements on human freedom because this subject, he felt, was a very obscure one:

> For there are some secret places in the Holy Scriptures into which God has not wished us to penetrate more deeply and, if we try to do so, then the deeper we go, the darker and darker it becomes, by which means we are led to acknowledge the unsearchable majesty of the divine wisdom, and the weakness of the human mind.[8]

Echoing Chrysostom's remark about the things that are "necessary," Erasmus argues that just a few things are "needful to know" about the doctrine of free choice and that it is irreverent to "rush into those things which are hidden, not to say superfluous." Then follows an important statement that could be interpreted as an affirmation of the clarity of Scripture on those matters that are truly significant:

> There are some things which God has willed that we should contemplate, as we venerate himself, in mystic silence; and, moreover, there are many passages in the sacred volumes about which many commentators have made guesses, but no one has

---

[7] See E. G. Rupp et al., eds., *Luther and Erasmus: Free Will and Salvation* (Library of Christian Classics 17; Philadelphia: Westminster, 1969).

[8] Ibid., p. 38.

finally cleared up their obscurity: as the distinction between the divine persons, the conjunction of the divine and human nature in Christ, the unforgivable sin; yet there are other things which God has willed to be *most plainly evident,* and such are the precepts for the good life. This is the Word of God, which is not to be bought in the highest heaven, nor in distant lands overseas, but it is close at hand, in our mouth and in our heart. These truths must be learned by all, but the rest are more properly committed to God, and it is more religious to worship them, being unknown, than to discuss them, being insoluble.[9]

Finally, he argues that certain topics, even if they can be understood, should not be discussed in the presence of the "untutored multitude," who might find them offensive and damaging.

As we might expect, Luther contests Erasmus's claim in the strongest of terms:

But that in Scripture there are some things abstruse, and everything is not plain—this is an idea put about by the ungodly Sophists, with whose lips you also speak here, Erasmus; but they have never produced, nor can they produce, a single article to prove this mad notion of theirs. Yet with such a phantasmagoria Satan has frightened men away from reading the Sacred Writ, and has made Holy Scripture contemptible, in order to enable the plagues he has bred from philosophy to prevail in the Church.[10]

More important for our present purposes, however, is Luther's recognition that there *are* indeed certain kinds of obscurities in Scripture that require (as his words certainly imply) scholarly research:

I admit, of course, that there are many texts in the Scriptures that are obscure and abstruse, not because of the majesty of their subject matter, but because of our ignorance of their vocabulary and grammar; but these texts in no way hinder a knowledge of the subject matter of Scripture.

Luther defines "subject matter" as "the supreme mystery brought to light, namely, that Christ the Son of God has been

made man, that God is three and one, that Christ has suffered
for us and is to reign eternally." Having thus defined the focus
of his concern, Luther goes on:

> The subject matter of the Scriptures, therefore, is all quite
> accessible, even though some texts are still obscure owing to our
> ignorance of their terms. Truly it is stupid and impious, when
> we know that the subject matter of Scripture has all been placed
> in the clearest light, to call it obscure on account of a few obscure
> words. If the words are obscure in one place, yet they are plain in
> another; and it is one and the same theme, published quite openly
> to the whole world, which in the Scriptures is sometimes
> expressed in plain words, and sometimes *lies as yet hidden* in
> obscure words.[11]

His conviction that difficult passages are made clear by others
(a point that will occupy us again shortly) echoes Augustine's
teaching:

> Accordingly the Holy Spirit has, with admirable wisdom and
> care for our welfare, so arranged the Holy Scriptures as by the
> plainer passages to satisfy our hunger, and by the more obscure
> to stimulate our appetite. For almost nothing is dug out of those
> obscure passages which may not be found set forth in the plainest
> language elsewhere.[12]

One could argue that Erasmus and Luther were not really
at odds on the question of the clarity of Scripture: they both
affirmed such a doctrine with regard to its essential message.
They did differ, however, on how one defines that message;
moreover, the tone and basic thrust in Erasmus's essay naturally
lead one to distrust the ability of the common believer to

---

[11] Ibid., pp. 110–11 (my emphasis). Cf. Origen's remark: "If some time, as
you read the Scripture, you stumble over a thought, good in reality yet a stone
of stumbling and a rock of offence, lay the blame on yourself. For you must not
give up the hope that this stone of stumbling and this rock of offence do possess
meaning" (from Homily 39 on Jeremiah, quoted in Tollinton, *Selections,*
pp. 49–50).

[12] Augustine, *On Christian Doctrine* 2.6 (*NPNF* 2:537). On the notion of
Scripture as its own best interpreter, see further below (pp. 103–4).

understand the Bible. Luther's most fundamental concerns were diametrically opposed to that tendency.[13]

THE NEED FOR QUALIFICATIONS

We must remember, however, that Luther did not for a moment deny the limitations of the interpreter's knowledge. For one thing, Christians differ in their level of maturity; indeed, extensive ministry in the church is almost a prerequisite for correct interpretation:

> No-one can understand the Bucolics of Virgil who has not been a herdsman for five years; nor his Georgics unless he has labored for five years in the fields. In order to understand aright the epistles of Cicero a man must have been full twenty years in the public service of a great state. No one need fancy he has tasted Holy Scripture who has not ruled the churches for a hundred years with prophets, like Elijah and Elisha, with John the Baptist, Christ and the apostles.[14]

More to the point, the clarity of Scripture does not at all preclude the need for specialists who seek to bridge the gap that separates us from the languages and cultures of the biblical writers. Luther himself was a man of broad erudition and of fine philological skills. He could argue that "to expound Scripture, to interpret it rightly and to fight against those people who quote wrongly . . . cannot be done without knowledge of the languages."[15] The energies he expended on his translation of

---

[13] These comments are too simple; I have ignored other complicating factors in the debate that are not directly relevant to our purpose. It should also be noticed that, if Erasmus and Luther did indeed differ in their identification of the essential message of Scripture, that factor itself could be used as an objection against the clarity of Scripture: if the Bible is so clear, why could not Luther and Erasmus agree on its fundamental subject matter? Luther's likely response to this question may be inferred from the subsequent discussion.

[14] Wood, *Luther's Principles,* p. 16. This quotation comes from a note written by Luther two days before his death; cf. P. Stuhlmacher, *Vom Verstehen des Neuen Testaments: Eine Hermeneutik* (GNT Ergänzungsreihe 6; Göttingen: Vandenhoeck & Ruprecht, 1979), p. 98.

[15] Wood, *Luther's Principles,* p. 29. Wood notes Luther's attention to detail: on one occasion Luther and two of his helpers spent four days translating three lines in the Book of Job (ibid.).

the Bible are the clearest testimonial to his conviction that the common folk did, in an important sense, depend on the expertise of scholars.

In any case, it would be a misunderstanding of the Reformers to interpret their emphasis on the perspicuity of Scripture in such a way as to make biblical scholarship unnecessary or unimportant. Developments in the various relevant disciplines during the last century or two heighten our sense of dependence on the careful work of scholars, yet at the same time such developments ought to increase our confidence that the Bible is not a locked mystery box but an accessible book that continues to open up its truths to those willing to search them out.

The essence of the Protestant position is captured well by the Westminster Confession of Faith (1647). The first chapter of that document contains a full statement regarding the character of Scripture, and paragraph 7 addresses directly the doctrine of perspicuity:

> All things in Scripture are not alike plain in themselves, nor alike clear unto all; yet those things which are necessary to be known, believed, and observed for salvation, are so clearly propounded, and opened in some place of Scripture or other, that not only the learned, but the unlearned, in a due use of the ordinary means, may attain unto a sufficient understanding of them.

Here the confession achieves a remarkable balance in its formulation. The emphasis falls heavily on the clarity of the biblical message, but the framers have been careful to qualify the doctrine in several ways: (1) not every part of Scripture is equally clear; (2) the matters in view are those that are necessary for salvation; (3) readers of the Bible must be willing to make use of "ordinary means"—personal study, fellowship with other believers, attention to the preaching of the Word; and (4) the interpreter's understanding will not be complete but will certainly be "sufficient" for the purpose stated.

One should notice, incidentally, the phrase "nor alike clear unto all." This qualification reminds us of the relative obscurity to be found in the minds of individual readers, a topic that occupies a prominent place in Luther's work. Luther was well aware that to acknowledge incidental obscurities in the text of Scripture did not fully address the problem raised by Erasmus. Accordingly, Luther goes on to deal with an additional factor.

> It is true that for many people much remains abstruse; but this is not due to the obscurity of Scripture, but to the blindness or indolence of those who will not take the trouble to look at the very clearest truth. [Here he quotes 2 Cor. 3:15 and 4:3–4.] . . . Let miserable men, therefore, stop imputing with blasphemous perversity the darkness and obscurity of their hearts to the wholly clear Scriptures of God.

As he comes to the end of this discussion, Luther summarizes his doctrine by pointing out that there are two kinds of clarity and two kinds of obscurity:

> one external and pertaining to the ministry of the Word, the other located in the understanding of the heart. If you speak of the internal clarity, no man perceives one iota of what is in the Scriptures unless he has the Spirit of God. . . . For the Spirit is required for the understanding of Scripture, both as a whole and in any part of it. If, on the other hand, you speak of the external clarity, nothing at all is left obscure or ambiguous, but everything there is in the Scriptures has been brought out by the Word into the most definite light, and published to all the world.[16]

HUMAN DARKNESS AND THE SPIRIT'S LIGHT

Luther's emphasis on the darkness of the human heart is nothing new, of course. We saw how significant this principle was in the medieval development of allegorical interpretation. It may be useful, moreover, to remind ourselves of Origen's conception that part of the divine aim was to conceal truth. We should not be too quick to condemn Origen, since he could

---

[16]Rupp, *Luther and Erasmus,* pp. 111–12; cf. Ralph A. Bohlmann, *Principles of Biblical Interpretation in the Lutheran Confessions,* rev. ed. (St. Louis: Concordia, 1983), pp. 53–63.

have easily appealed to several important passages of Scripture in support of his view.

For example, even if we allow for some degree of literary hyperbole in Isaiah 6:9–10, we cannot do justice to that passage unless we recognize that at least one aspect of Isaiah's mission was to darken the hearts of many Israelites.

> Go and tell this people:
> "Be ever hearing, but never understanding;
>   be ever seeing, but never perceiving."
> Make the heart of this people calloused;
>   make their ears dull
>   and close their eyes.
> Otherwise they might see with their eyes,
>   hear with their ears,
>   understand with their hearts,
> and turn and be healed.

This passage clearly speaks of divine retribution against those who have set themselves against the God of Israel. The point is developed from a different angle in 8:14–15, where the Lord describes himself, not only as a "sanctuary" (to believers), but also as

> a stone that causes men to stumble
>   and a rock that makes them fall.
> And for the people of Jerusalem he will be
>   a trap and a snare.
> Many of them will stumble;
>   they will fall and be broken,
>   they will be snared and captured.

These portions of Scripture became very important to the apostles as they sought to understand Israel's rejection of the gospel message. Jesus himself had appealed to Isaiah 6 in connection with his practice of speaking in parables. The relevant passage is Mark 4:10–12, one that itself has become quite a stone of stumbling to modern scholars, who think it is absurd to take Jesus' words in their apparent meaning. After all, parables are intended to illustrate and clarify a message! Why would our Lord say anything that was actually designed to keep people from understanding?[17]

In truth, however, Jesus' message had the same two-edged function as Isaiah's ministry: a blessing to believers and a curse to God's enemies. The elderly Simeon, as he held the baby Jesus in his arms, declared that Jesus was "destined to cause the falling and rising of many in Israel" (Luke 2:34). The apostle Paul described his message as a fragrance of life, the aroma of Christ for salvation, but he acknowledged that, to those who are perishing, it is "the smell of death" (2 Cor. 2:14–16). Not surprisingly, both Paul and Peter quote Isaiah 8:14 as they deal with the difficult problem of seeing many reject the message of the gospel (Rom. 9:32–33; 1 Peter 2:4–8; it should be noted that both of these passages have a very strong predestinarian motif).[18]

It was unfortunate that Origen should make the factor of God's concealing truth so basic in his hermeneutical system, but we dare not forget the principle altogether. Even those who have responded in faith to the divine message continue to be sinners. The corruption of sin will always affect our understanding of Scripture to a greater or lesser extent; part of our responsibility, therefore, is to learn to depend more and more on the illumination of the Holy Spirit.

We need to be careful, of course, not to use this blessing to justify our prejudices and laziness. The guidance of the Spirit does not preclude our making use of "the ordinary means" that the Westminster Confession refers to. Moreover, we need to appreciate that the passages that stress the role of the Spirit in interpreting God's message (one thinks primarily of 1 Cor. 2:6–14) do not focus on difficult exegetical details but precisely on those matters that are needful for salvation. Quite properly, therefore, the Westminster Confession reminds us: "Neverthe-

---

[17] According to C. F. D. Moule, it would be "perversely literalistic" to suggest "that parables are used *in order* to exclude" (*The Birth of the New Testament,* 3d rev. ed. [New York: Harper & Row, 1982], pp. 116–17).

[18] On the use of "stone" passages in the New Testament, see esp. Barnabas Lindars, *New Testament Apologetic: The Doctrinal Significance of the Old Testament Quotations* (London: SCM, 1961), pp. 169–86.

less, we acknowledge the inward illumination of the Spirit of God to be necessary *for the saving understanding* of such things as are revealed in the Word" (1. 6; my emphasis).

This factor helps us to deal with a troublesome matter: does it make sense to use commentaries written by unbelieving scholars? Why should we depend on the judgment of those whose hearts have not been enlightened by the ministry of the Spirit? The usual answer is that many of the issues modern commentators deal with do not directly affect Christian doctrine. Such a response, by itself, is not wholly satisfactory, yet there is enough truth in it to serve our present purposes. Even a heart deeply antagonistic to the gospel does not lead a scholar to identify a noun as a verb. Leaning on the expertise of scholars who have specialized interests should be regarded as one more instance of using "ordinary means" in the study of Scripture.

This perspective can help us make sense of a frequently cited verse that is both reassuring and puzzling: "As for you, the anointing you received from him remains in you, and you do not need anyone to teach you" (1 John 2:27). Some Christians tend to absolutize this statement and to resist the notion that scholarly work is helpful and important. They forget, of course, that they cannot even read the Bible without depending on the scholarly work that has made Bible translations possible. *Someone* had to learn Greek and Hebrew; *someone* had to study ancient culture; *someone* had to develop expertise in transferring the message of the original to clear, forceful English—all of which had to happen before modern American believers could claim that they need no one to teach them about the Bible!

THE ROLE OF SCHOLARSHIP

We do indeed need help not at all because the Scriptures are inherently obscure but because we are far removed from the biblical writers in time and culture. Even a document written carefully in clearly formulated English, such as the Declaration of Independence, can *appear* obscure two hundred years later. The very opening phrase, "When in the course of human events. . . ," will be partially lost to a modern reader who does not realize that the word *course* carried some strong philosophical nuances in the eighteenth century.[19] What shall we say, then, about a document written not two hundred but two thousand years ago? not in English but in very different languages? not in America but in the Mediterranean world?

The history of biblical interpretation during the past century or two—whatever objectionable features it has had—must be understood primarily as an attempt to bridge this massive linguistic and cultural gap between us and the original text. The development of highly specialized critical tools may appear to create a wall between the simple believer and the Bible, but in effect it facilitates bringing the two together. Not all scholars, of course, view their work in this way—and many who do often fail to meet such a goal. Furthermore, modern critical approaches should not be viewed naïvely as completely neutral with respect to the question of faith.[20] A believing scholar must bring any hermeneutical approach (even those developed by evangelical scholars!) under the searching light of Scripture itself.

In spite of such qualifications, we can state unequivocally that modern biblical scholarship has helped to open up the meaning of innumerable passages of Scripture, sometimes in very dramatic ways. The discovery and analysis of the Egyptian papyri, for example, has increased our understanding of New Testament Greek almost beyond reckoning. The development

---

[19] Gary Wills, *Inventing America: Jefferson's Declaration of Independence* (Garden City, N.Y.: Doubleday, 1978), p. 93 and chap. 8.

[20] Cf. Troeltsch's views mentioned above in chap. 2. The most significant contribution to this fundamental question is the controversial thesis of the "twofold division of science," propounded by Abraham Kuyper (*Encyclopedia,* pp. 150–82). Though in many respects believing and unbelieving science have the same character, argued Kuyper, they move in different directions because of their different starting points (p. 155). Cornelius Van Til has insisted on the same point in many of his writings; see *A Christian Theory of Knowledge* (n.p.: Presbyterian and Reformed, 1969), pp. 21–22 and passim. For an attempt to develop the implications of this thesis, see Gary North, ed., *Foundations of Christian Scholarship: Essays in the Van Til Perspective* (Vallecito, Calif.: Ross House, 1976).

of Old Testament form criticism, though it has spun many questionable and radical theories, has made it possible for us to uncover the significance of various kinds of literary genres within the Hebrew Bible.[21] And so on and on.

We dare not confuse, therefore, the peculiar and often harmful proposals of radical scholars with the actual advances of biblical scholarship as a whole. Someone committed to the authority of Scripture and convinced that those proposals must be rejected can still recognize the enormous contribution of modern scholarship to the understanding of the Bible.[22]

If we think that nowadays we face more exegetical problems than earlier generations did, the reason is precisely that we know more about the Bible and therefore have a greater awareness of our ignorance. Two hundred years ago, Bible readers only thought that they understood many passages that now we have doubts about. Paradoxically, our *subjective sense* of the clarity of Scripture seems diminished at the same time that we have *greater objective evidence* regarding the clear meaning of the Bible. To recognize this fact is to remind ourselves that we cannot confuse what Luther called the external and internal aspects of the doctrine of scriptural perspicuity. We dare not attribute to Scripture the limitations of our minds and hearts.

Even more to the point, however, is our need to appreciate that all of the advances in modern scholarship—and all of the new questions raised by it—do not affect the basic outlines of Christian theology. Many individual scholars, of course, reject the great doctrines of the Reformation on the basis of modern philosophical commitments.[23] But changes in

---

[21] In addition to the well-known research of A. Deissmann, J. H. Moulton, and others at the beginning of the century, see the recent work by G. H. R. Horsley, *New Documents Illustrating Early Christianity* (North Ryde, N.S.W.: Macquarie University, 1981–). See also Tremper Longman III, "Form Criticism, Recent Developments in Genre Theory, and the Evangelical," *WTJ* 47 (1985): 46–67.

[22] It is ironic that wrong-headed and obnoxious theories very often sensitize responsible scholars to valid questions that would otherwise not have occurred to them. See my article "The Place of Historical Reconstruction in New Testament Criticism," pp. 122–33.

[23] In particular, many scholars have adopted a thoroughgoing naturalism. Useful surveys documenting the development of biblical scholarship during the

our understanding of individual passages of Scripture do not require or even suggest that we alter the essence of the Christian message.

Referring again to the Westminster Confession of Faith, perhaps the most comprehensive theological statement arising from the Reformation, we may ask: Is there any chapter in that document that needs revision because we now conclude that, say, the Song of Solomon was written, not as an allegory, but as a description of human love? Is there even a paragraph that must now be excised because of advances in textual criticism or philology? The answer is a definitive and unequivocal no.

Neither this document nor any other theological confession is perfect; we must recognize that Christians have grown in their understanding of Scripture and may indeed wish to revise certain aspects of any doctrinal statement. But all of the increased knowledge and sophistication of the modern era does not suggest for a moment that previous generations of Christians misunderstood the gospel message.

THE WHOLE COUNSEL OF GOD

The reason for such stability in the face of dramatic advancement is that the great teachings of Scripture are not dependent on the interpretation of any particular verse in isolation from others. Though Christians sometimes rely heavily on certain proof texts, the church has come to understand the divine message by developing sensitivity to the *consistent* teaching of the Bible *as a whole*.

The believer is thus not at all a slave to scholarly pronouncements. Believers may express puzzlement and even distress upon hearing a new interpretation of some favorite text, but they will usually adjust to it if they can eventually see how it fits their understanding of Scripture as a whole. What they will not tolerate—and rightly so—is an interpretation that obvi-

---

past two centuries are the essays by W. Neil and A. Richardson in *CHB* 3:238–338. For greater detail on the development of British views on Scripture, see the highly regarded work by H. G. Reventlow, *The Authority of the Bible and the Rise of the Modern World* (Philadelphia: Fortress, 1984).

ously conflicts with the consistent tenor of the biblical teaching. In the most fundamental sense, believers need no one to teach them (1 John 2:27), and the most imposing scholarship will not intimidate them.

A most interesting sidelight to this discussion is the fact that even Origen justified his hermeneutical program along lines similar to those we have been considering. At one point, after acknowledging the validity of the literal meaning, he argued that we have the need and responsibility, not merely to grasp the sense of any given passage, but to assimilate the *entire* meaning of Scripture.[24] Origen did not expand on this idea, and perhaps we should not make too much of it, but he apparently maintained a strong sense of the importance of contextual interpretation. Because of the unity of the Bible, the whole of Scripture constitutes the context to any one passage, and Christians who are spiritually mature may be expected to draw all the threads together. We make a serious mistake if we do not see this process as an essential aspect of allegorical interpretation. And what was true of Origen was certainly true of the Fathers in general:

> They knew what was their aim in handling scripture. It was not to produce an entirely consistent system of doctrine which would somehow fit in every little detail of the Bible, nor was it to set up a biblical literalism which would treat the Bible as one treats a railway timetable. It was to discover, and to preach and teach, the burden, the purport, the drift, the central message of the Bible.[25]

[24] Origen, *On First Principles* 4. 3. 5, pp. 296–97. Wiles asked, from a somewhat different perspective, what criteria controlled a method as flexible as that of allegory: "An important part of the answer to that question is Origen's conviction that scripture must always be consistent with itself, that the real meaning of every passage will be part of the truth of the one Christian faith" ("Origen," pp. 479–80).

[25] Hanson, "Biblical Exegesis," p. 452. On the same issue, see Michael Andrew Fahey, *Cyprian and the Bible: A Study in Third-Century Exegesis* (BGBH 9; Tübingen: J. C. B. Mohr, 1971), p. 473. The great Charles Spurgeon, in spite of his questionable use of certain texts as the basis for his sermons, was kept from distorting the biblical message through his impressive familiarity with the overall teaching of Scripture.

A corresponding principle vigorously formulated at the time of the Reformation is that Scripture is its best interpreter. We earlier noticed that Luther appealed to this notion in response to the charge that there are obscurities in the Bible ("If the words are obscure in one place, yet they are plain in another"). As early as the second century, Irenaeus articulated this principle when he argued against certain gnostic views:

> For no question can be solved by means of another which itself waits solution; nor, in the opinion of those possessed of sense, can an ambiguity be explained by means of another ambiguity, or enigmas by means of another greater enigma, but things of such character receive their solution from those which are manifest, and consistent, and clear.[26]

Oddly, Farrar objects to the idea that "Scripture interprets itself, a rule which exegetically considered has no meaning."[27] Quite the opposite, this rule is the most fundamental hermeneutical principle when dealing with any piece of literature; it is, in effect, the principle of contextual interpretation. Anyone who views God as the author of Scripture can hardly afford to ignore it.

CHURCH AND TRADITION

One final problem requires our attention in this chapter—the question that we raised earlier concerning submissiveness to the teaching of the church. How does the clarity of Scripture relate to this question? Should we depend on the church to teach us about the Scripture?

For that matter, what is the role of tradition? The

---

[26] Irenaeus, *Against Heresies* 2. 10. 1 (*ANF* 1:370); cf. de Margerie, *Introduction* 1:70, who also refers to 2. 10. 2 and 3. 27. 1 and to Salvator Herrera, *Saint Irénée de Lyon exégète* (Paris: A. Savieta, 1920), pp. 120ff. Origen also held to this principle; see Hanson, *Allegory,* p. 180.

[27] Farrar, *History,* p. 332, n. 1. He does observe, however, that the watchword *analogia fidei* is a wise one insofar as it forbids us "to isolate and distort any one passage into authoritative contradiction to the whole tenor of Scripture" (p. 333). Cf. the positive treatment in Bohlmann, *Principles,* chap. 6.

Protestant Reformation is usually characterized as a massive break with tradition. There is a very important element of truth in that characterization, but here again a crucial caveat is necessary. The Reformers opposed the authority of tradition and of the church, but *only insofar as this authority usurped the authority of Scripture.* They never rejected the value of the church's exegetical tradition when it was used in submission to the Scriptures.

> Luther could not have been the exegete he was without the help of the church's tradition. The tradition gave him a footing on which he could and did move and shift, but which he never lost. But this was so because he believed that under this footing was the foundation of the Scriptures themselves, which he, as an expositor of the Scriptures and also as a son of the church, was to receive gratefully. . . . Luther knew the difference between gratitude and idolatry in the reception of the church's heritage. In this sense he advanced the audacious claim that by his exposition of the Scriptures he was a most loyal defender of the tradition, and that the idolatrous traditionalism of his opponents could mean the eventual destruction both of Scripture and of tradition.[28]

Consider in this regard John Calvin's development. Calvin had no peer in the sixteenth century as an expositor of Scripture, but he was under no illusion that he could somehow skip a millennium and a half of exegetical tradition and approach the Bible free from the influence of the past. The first edition of his *Institutes of the Christian Religion* appeared in 1536, when Calvin was only in his twenties. Enlarged editions appeared in 1539 and 1541 and more significant alterations beginning in 1543, but the work did not reach its final form until 1559. During these two decades Calvin was immersed in biblical exposition and preaching. "As his understanding of the Bible broadened and deepened, so the subject matter of the Bible demanded ever new understanding in its interrelations

---

[28] Jaroslav Pelikan, *Luther the Expositor: Introduction to the Reformer's Exegetical Writings* (companion vol. to *Luther's Works*; St. Louis: Concordia, 1959), p. 88.

within itself, in its relations with secular philosophy, in its *interpretation by previous commentators*."[29]

This last point is most important, for Calvin also spent considerable time studying the major theologians of the church. Indeed, beginning with the 1543 edition, there were "vastly increased" references to the Fathers, including Augustine, Ambrose, Cyprian, Theodoret, and others.[30] Calvin's position was well thought out:

> Insofar as possible, we should hold to the work of earlier exegetes. The Reformer saw himself as bound by and indebted to the exegetical tradition of the church, above all the early church, especially Augustine. He was unwilling to give up the consensus of interpretation.[31]

It is clear, then, that the Reformation marked a break with the *abuse* of tradition but not with the tradition itself. This fact tells us a great deal about the Reformers' sense of corporate identity with the Christian church as a whole. It would not have occurred to them to interpret the Scripture as autonomous individuals. On the contrary, they were most forceful in their interpretations when they were convinced that they were giving expression to the truth *given to the church*.

Unfortunately, some would have us believe that the genius of the Reformation was a breaking loose from authority in general and that post-Enlightenment biblical critics, in their radical abandonment of church guidance and scriptural authority, were really giving more consistent expression to the fundamental principle of the Reformation.[32] Disturbing too is the fact that even conservative scholars in our day sometimes give much higher priority to individualism than to corporate responsibility. The idea of pursuing truth "wherever it may lead

---

[29] T. H. L. Parker, *John Calvin: A Biography* (Philadelphia: Westminster, 1975), p. 132, my emphasis.

[30] Ibid., p. 106.

[31] Kraus, "Calvin's Exegetical Principles," p. 11. Note also Peter Stuhlmacher, *Historical Criticism and Theological Interpretation of Scripture: Toward a Hermeneutics of Consent* (Philadelphia: Fortress, 1977), pp. 34–35.

[32] Troeltsch's thesis clearly implies this view; note Harvey, *Historian and Believer*, pp. 3–9.

us" becomes a pious but misconceived motto, for truth rarely if ever manifests itself in isolation.

No doubt there are cases when a scholar hits on an idea whose time has not come, and the fact that the church is not immediately convinced of its validity is no reason to abandon it altogether. On the other hand, new theories and strange interpretations have been suggested by the thousands, most of them never to be propounded again. The humble believer who, innocent of historical and critical methods, cannot see how these interpretations fit in with the church's understanding of the truth may thereby show greater perception of the meaning of Scripture. In a paradoxical way, the clarity of Scripture thus proves triumphant over the misguided attempts of human wisdom, and Jesus' prayer finds a new application: "I praise you, Father, Lord of heaven and earth, because you have hidden these things from the wise and learned, and revealed them to little children. Yes, Father, for this was your good pleasure" (Matt. 11:25–26).

5

RELATIVE OR ABSOLUTE?

The fact that we encounter a variety of difficulties in our efforts to understand the Bible can be troubling to believers. If biblical interpretation is a *human* and therefore fallible activity, can any such interpretation be trustworthy? A related, but distinct, question has been raised in modern times by writers who doubt whether "objective" interpretation is at all possible. Strongly influenced by a Kantian world view, they argue that our perception of the world is basically determined by our subjective preconceptions. In a very important sense, according to this viewpoint, the past is really lost to us; therefore, we do not merely interpret past events and statements—we recreate them in our image. This way of thinking, if applied consistently, would certainly do away with the usual approach to biblical interpretation.

One other problem involves the claim that, not only our interpretation, but the biblical text itself must be viewed as relative. Such an objection cannot simply be ignored. Though we accept the divine origin and therefore absolute authority of the Scriptures, it is still true that the divine message is couched in human language and that it addresses specific historical and cultural situations, some of which have changed considerably in the course of time. Even the most conservative Christians recognize that at least some commands of Scripture cannot or need not be applied literally in our day, though there is plenty of disagreement as to which belong in this category (footwashing? length of women's hair? eating pork? muzzling the ox while it treads?). Does this fact relativize the Bible and compromise its absolute authority?

These questions bring us to the modern debate over *contextualization*.[1] This term has become suspect in the minds of many Christians because it is sometimes used to justify far-reaching changes in the proclamation of the gospel. Some have suggested, for example, that, since Muslims have a very negative view of baptism (due to historical associations), a proper contextualizing of the gospel in Islamic culture may require replacing this rite with some other.

It would be a mistake, however, to jettison the basic concept of contextualization simply because it has been abused. The fact is that every attempt we make at understanding the Bible (or any other ancient document) necessarily involves transferring a particular text from one historical context to another. When contemporary Christians read a portion of Scripture (already partially contextualized by the English version!), they can make sense of it only from the context of their own knowledge and experience.

The question, therefore, is not *whether* we should contextualize, for we all do it, but rather, *how* to do it without compromising the integrity of the Bible. Does the history of interpretation give us any help here?

INTERPRETATION IN ISRAEL AND IN JUDAISM

We should remind ourselves that the history of biblical

---

[1] This topic is more properly treated in the last volume of the series. I deal with it here only as it affects the general question of cultural relativity. For some preliminary bibliography, see the articles by J. Robertson McQuilkin and David J. Hesselgrave in *HIB*, pp. 219–40 and 693–738. Note also Ramesh P. Richard, "Methodological Proposals for Scripture Relevance," *BSac* 143 (1986): 14–23, 123–33, 205–17. At the center of the debate has been the work by Charles H. Kraft, *Christianity and Culture: A Study in Dynamic Biblical Theologizing in Cross-Cultural Perspective* (Maryknoll, N.Y.: Orbis, 1979).

interpretation begins with the biblical writings themselves; not surprisingly, therefore, we find examples of contextualization within the pages of Scripture. One particularly beautiful instance is the way Psalm 16 appears to use Numbers 18:20, "Then the LORD said to Aaron, 'You shall have no inheritance in their land, nor own any portion among them; I am your portion and your inheritance among the sons of Israel'" (NASB; Deut. 18:1–2 speaks similarly of the Levites in general). It has been suggested, with some plausibility, that Psalm 16 was written by David at a time when he was forced to leave the Promised Land. Because the worship of the God of Israel was tied so closely to the inheritance of that land, abandoning one meant abandoning the other (cf. David's words in 1 Sam. 26:19). Whether or not Psalm 16 has this actual setting, David clearly had learned a profound lesson. He would not abandon the God of Israel. He could appropriate God's promise to the Levites: "The LORD is the portion of my inheritance and my cup; Thou dost support my lot. The lines have fallen to me in pleasant places; indeed, my heritage is beautiful to me" (Ps. 16:5–6 NASB).

Some may object that, strictly speaking, this example is not so much one of biblical interpretation as one of *application*.[2] The point here is of the greatest importance. The classic grammatico-historical method of interpretation insists precisely that a clear-cut distinction be maintained between exegesis (the biblical author's intended meaning at the time of writing) and application (the meaning, or significance, to the reader now). That distinction lies at the basis of virtually every interpretive advance made in the past couple of centuries, and we dare not undermine it.

Unfortunately, this is the very point at issue in the contemporary debate: is it really possible to exegete a text without appropriating it into the present? Note the fundamental

---

[2]In criticism of appeals to *sensus plenior*, for example, Walter C. Kaiser, Jr., speaks of those who confuse "the necessary work of the Holy Spirit in illumination, application, and personally applying a text with the original scope and content of that text in the singular act of revelation to the writer" (*The Uses of the Old Testament in the New Testament* [Chicago: Moody, 1985], p. 28).

difference between this question and the godly concern to apply Scripture to our daily lives. All believers recognize that exegesis should not remain merely an intellectual and antiquarian task: it ought to bear fruit in the present. The contemporary claim, however, is not that exegesis *ought* to be applied but that, in the very nature of the case, it is always applied, that we fool ourselves if we think we can formulate a biblical writer's meaning apart from the significance his writing has for us.

Interestingly, recent attempts to identify the character of Jewish exegesis, or *midrash,* focus precisely on the people's need to *actualize* the revealed Word of God.[3] Once again, we could point out many examples of this approach from within the Old Testament itself, such as Isaiah's use of the Exodus motif, the Chronicler's rewriting of the Samuel-Kings narrative, and so on.

Of special interest is the development of biblical interpretation during the intertestamental period, for the Jewish people were faced with the need to understand afresh the requirements of the law in view of their new cultural situation. An intense desire to obey that law in all its concreteness led to a growing body of interpretive tradition, the so-called Oral Law, which in course of time achieved its own authoritative status. Jesus spoke of these "traditions of the elders" as objectionable teachings of men that had the effect of annulling the word of God. Our Lord, of course, rebuked the Pharisees not for seeking to understand and apply the Scriptures but for allowing human interpretations—that is, their contextualizations—to be placed on a par with the divine revelation. The consequence of their hermeneutics was often to violate the commands of God.[4]

---

[3] Particularly influential has been an article by R. Bloch, "Midrash," reprinted in *Approaches to Judaism: Theory and Practice,* ed. W. S. Green (Brown Judaic Studies 1; Missoula, Mont.: Scholars Press, 1978), pp. 29–50. Warnings against the ambiguity of the term are commonplace. Helpful in this regard is Gary Porton, "Defining Midrash," in *The Ancient Study of Judaism,* 2 vols., ed. J. Neusner (n.p.: Ktav, 1981) 1:5–92; see also "Bibliography on Midrash" by Lee Haas on pp. 93–103. Worthy of special note is the literate study by Barry W. Holtz, "Midrash," in *Back to the Sources: Reading the Classic Jewish Texts,* ed. B. W. Holtz (New York: Summit Books, 1984), pp. 177–211.

[4] Note especially Mark 7:1–13. See my article "The Place of Historical Reconstruction," pp. 112–21.

A separatist Jewish group, the community at Qumran, affords another notable example of how the Bible could be actualized. In their case the dominant concept was eschatological, a conviction that they were living in the last days, that many biblical passages were being fulfilled in their midst, and that they themselves would be God's instrument for the consummation of history. Their famous Habakkuk commentary, for instance, consists of running short citations from that prophet, followed usually by the term *pishro* ("its interpretation [is]"), which introduces their explanation of the text. Invariably, the explanation involves the identification of the biblical statements with people and events somehow related to the Qumran community. A typical case is their commentary on Habakkuk 2:17 ("The violence you have done to Lebanon will overwhelm you, and your destruction of animals [or "livestock"] will terrify you"):

> [The interpretation of the passage (*pishro*)] concerns the Wicked Priest [an enemy of the Qumran community], by heaping upon him the same recompense which he heaped upon the poor—for "Lebanon" is the Council of the Community; and the "livestock" are the simple of Judah the Law Doer—for God will condemn him to destruction, in as much as he plotted to destroy the poor.[5]

This exegetical method has come to be known as *pesher-*interpretation.

Students of the New Testament will recognize a certain parallel between the concerns of the Qumranites and the teaching of Jesus and his apostles. When the Dead Sea Scrolls were discovered, some writers raised the possibility that the New Testament message was in some way dependent on the Qumran tradition. That suggestion has long since been

---

[5] W. H. Brownlee, *The Midrash Pesher of Habakkuk* (SBLMS 24; Missoula, Mont.: Scholars Press, 1979), p. 196. Brownlee translates *pesher* as "the prophetic fulfillment." Note also F. F. Bruce, "Biblical Exposition at Qumran," in *Gospel Perspectives*, vol. 4, *Studies in Midrash and Historiography*, ed. R. T. France and D. Wenham (Sheffield: JSOT, 1983), pp. 77–98, and G. J. Brooke, *Exegesis at Qumran: 4QFlorilegium in Its Jewish Context* (JSOT Supp. 29; Sheffield: JSOT, 1985).

discredited, but some of the parallels continue to be illuminating. Our Lord's proclamation that the kingdom of heaven was at hand, the many references in the Gospels to the fulfillment of prophecy, Paul's allusion to the revelation of the long-hidden "mystery" (Col. 1:26–27; cf. 1 Cor. 2:7–10), and various other statements (e.g., 1 Cor. 10:11; Heb. 1:2; 9:26) make clear that the New Testament writers approached the Old Testament from an eschatological perspective.

THE RIDDLE OF MESSIANIC PROPHECY

Our discussion so far may raise a new question: Is the interpretation of prophecy by the New Testament writers another instance of "contextualization"? This is a most difficult problem. A positive answer might suggest that Old Testament prophecies were not truly predictive, while a negative answer implies that those prophecies had little or no relevance for the original recipients.

For example, Isaiah's prophecy that the virgin would conceive and give birth to Immanuel (7:14) may be taken as purely predictive of Jesus' birth. But many scholars object that such a use of that verse wrenches the statement out of its historical and literary context; that is, the Immanuel prophecy sounds in its setting like something to be fulfilled in the very near future. But emphasis on this historical aspect could easily lead us to take Matthew's quotation (1:22–23) as a mere application of an ancient event to the birth of Jesus, and Evangelicals understandably tend to react strongly against such an approach. Unfortunately, it is very easy to overreact, and as a result the original context of the prophecy is often overlooked.

To complicate matters further, we need to consider whether the prophet himself would have been conscious of the explicitly messianic character of his statements. Conservatives have often handled this question by appealing to the divine origin of those prophecies. In other words, perhaps the prophets sometimes did not really know that they were predicting certain messianic events, but God did know, and this knowledge is revealed in the New Testament.

Other conservatives would argue, however, that this way of looking at the problem is fundamentally unsound—that the only way to find out what God means in Scripture is to identify what the *human writers* themselves meant. Any ad hoc appeal to God's intention (as distinguishable from the biblical writers' intention) in effect undermines grammatico-historical exegesis, which is the only sound method of understanding the Bible.[6]

The relation between this topic and that of allegorical interpretation is obvious, since the messianic interpretation of prophecy appears to see something "extra" in the text. Moreover, as we have noted, the allegorical method was motivated by the need for relevance, while in this chapter we are considering the use of Old Testament passages by later individuals who wished to actualize those texts.

Christians have for centuries been exercised about the messianic predictions in the Old Testament. Theodore of Mopsuestia, reacting to the Alexandrian approach, minimized this element. Though he did believe that Old Testament prophecies were predictive, he argued that they were normally fulfilled within the Old Testament period itself. In such a view, one finds in the New Testament use of those passages

> free and coherent accommodations of the original texts to analogous settings in the Christian revelation. The Old Testament texts, he held, lent themselves to this use because of their

---

[6]Note Daniel P. Fuller, "Interpretation, History of," *ISBE* 2:863–74, esp. the end of the article. Particularly forceful in expressing this point of view is Walter C. Kaiser; see his *Uses,* pp. 17–22, in which he deals in detail with 1 Peter 1:10–12. On p. 71 he appeals to the Antiochene concept of *theōria,* a matter that will occupy us presently. Darrell L. Bock has attempted a classification of viewpoints on this question; see his "Evangelicals and the Use of the Old Testament in the New," *BSac* 142 (1985): 209–23, 306–19. By far the best treatment of the relation between the divine and the human elements in biblical interpretation is Vern S. Poythress, "Divine Meaning of Scripture," *WTJ* 48 (1986): 241–79. For an interesting contrast between two opposing ways of handling the Psalms, see the articles by Bruce K. Waltke and Walter C. Kaiser, Jr., in *Tradition and Testament: Essays in Honor of Charles Lee Feinberg,* ed. John S. Feinberg and Paul D. Feinberg (Chicago: Moody, 1981), pp. 3–37.

"hyperbolical" imagery and blessings, rich in metaphorical meaning, and phraseological symbolism.[7]

Centuries later, medieval interpreters, influenced by the Jewish emphasis on literal exegesis, could not always account for the messianic element. As distinguished a scholar as Andrew of St. Victor could actually read Isaiah 53 without reference to Christ![8] Even Calvin, for that matter, could not avoid being affected by this trend: Farrar proudly points to Calvin's interpretation of messianic Psalms as a genuine anticipation of the "modern" method.[9]

Opponents of Christianity have often focused on this problem. The eighteenth-century skeptic Anthony Collins argued that there were only two options available to Christians: literal or nonliteral interpretation. If the literal method is accepted, one thereby falsifies the New Testament use of the Old Testament. If one accepts a nonliteral approach, then any interpretation is possible, and the whole operation becomes meaningless.[10]

How can we respond to these challenges? Is it possible to do full justice to the original setting of the messianic prophecies without compromising their predictive element? One important item on the agenda of evangelical biblical scholarship is to demonstrate that the answer is yes.

To begin with, we need to remind ourselves that early Christian interpreters did not sharply distinguish between the meaning intended by the human author and that intended by God. In the Antiochene concept of *theōria*, the prophet's (but

---

[7] Zaharopoulos, "Theodore of Mopsuestia's Critical Methods," p. 228. On p. 230 he states that even typological interpretation "is almost completely absent" in Theodore's system.

[8] Smalley, *Study of the Bible,* p. 165.

[9] Farrar, *History*; pp. 346–47, 472. It should be obvious by now that the hermeneutical problem of the Old Testament—underlined by the use that the New Testament writers make of it—is the central and foundational interpretive issue that the church has had to wrestle with throughout the centuries. The point comes out clearly in the brief article by J. N. S. Alexander, "Interpretation of Scripture in the Ante-Nicene Period," *Int* 12 (1958): 272–80.

[10] Frei, *Eclipse,* p. 70.

also the interpreter's) "vision" encompasses more than what is immediately evident.[11] But even Eusebius, who was very capable of Origenistic allegorizing, would have agreed.

> The definition of the literal sense as the sense intended by the author, independently of the nature of its object, and the spiritual sense as the one intended by the Holy Ghost, but of which the prophet was unconscious, is inapplicable to the exegesis of Eusebius, and obviously of all the Fathers of the early centuries. Such dichotomy of the Biblical sense was unknown to them.[12]

Moreover, we should consider the possibility that fulfilled prophecy and contextualization (or application?) are not mutually exclusive ideas. One can hardly deny that the original audience that heard the Immanuel prophecies would have naturally assumed some kind of fulfillment within their lifetime (specifically, the coming of the Assyrians before the child was to grow up; see Isa. 7:16–17 and cf. 8:6–8). These same hearers, however, must surely have been impressed by the increasing greatness ascribed to this figure in the subsequent prophecies (9:1–7; 11:1–16). Without ignoring the historical situation of the original hearers, God was certainly stretching their horizons, that is, awakening them to the fact that the prophecies ultimately transcended their limited perspective.

The fact that the New Testament writers make no reference to the original situation when they quote these and other prophecies does not imply that they would have denied their historical significance. If this is correct, then it would be

---

[11] For a clear discussion of this approach and how it compares with the Alexandrian method, note Raymond E. Brown, *The Sensus Plenior of Scripture* (Baltimore: St. Mary's University, 1955), pp. 45–51. A helpful summary of the modern discussion may be found in de Margerie, *Introduction* 1:188–213. For a translation of the relevant passages in Diodore of Tarsus, see Froehlich, *Biblical Interpretation,* pp. 82–94.

[12] Carmel Sant, *The Old Testament Interpretation of Eusebius of Caesarea: The Manifold Sense of Holy Scripture* (Malta: Royal University of Malta, 1967), p. 119. For the Fathers, he continues, the literal and spiritual senses refer to two "orders of reality forming one object of the prophetic vision, hence both of them were intended and expressed by the writer." See also Wallace-Hadrill, *Eusebius,* pp. 83, 96–97; Kerrigan, *Cyril,* p. 234.

appropriate to say that they were contextualizing those passages to the new situation created by the coming of Christ. On the other hand, it would be a blatant fallacy to deduce that the apostles did not regard the prophecies as straightforward, supernatural predictions. In other words, there is no evidence that the early Christians made a sharp distinction between the fulfillment of prophecy and the actualizing of Scripture.

The point may be illustrated from Isaiah 52:15, "For what [nations and kings] were not told, they will see, and what they have not heard, they will understand." This statement is part of the prophecy regarding the Suffering Servant, itself part of a series of passages regarding a "servant" that seems at times identified with the prophet himself, at other times with the nation of Israel as a whole, and at still other times with the Messiah to come (cf. 42:14; 44:1; 49:3–6). It cannot be doubted that the New Testament writers saw these prophecies fulfilled in the coming of Jesus Christ, yet Paul has no misgivings about applying Isaiah 52:15 *to his own ministry* among the Gentiles (Rom. 15:20–21).[13]

ANCIENT COMMANDS IN A MODERN WORLD

Even more clearly than for prophecy, the significance of numerous other passages of Scripture shifted from their original setting as later circumstances themselves changed.[14] It is a logical equivocation, however, to say that this concept "relativizes" the Bible so as to deprive it of its authority. The divine authority of Scripture comes to human beings in their concrete

[13] Paul "acted in the spirit of the prediction that Christ should be preached where He had not been known. . . . There is, however, no objection to considering this passage as merely an expression, in borrowed language, of the apostle's own ideas" (Charles Hodge, *Commentary on the Epistle to the Romans* [Grand Rapids: Eerdmans, 1964; orig. 1886], p. 441). See also my article, "The New Testament Use of the Old Testament: Text-Form and Authority," in *Scripture and Truth,* ed. D. A. Carson and J. D. Woodbridge (Grand Rapids: Zondervan, 1983), pp. 147–65, esp. p. 158.

[14] In addition to the bibliographical items mentioned in n. 1 above, see Harvey M. Conn, *Eternal Word and Changing Worlds,* esp. chaps. 5 and 8, and his article "Normativity, Relevance and Relativity," *TSF Bulletin* 10 (1987): 24–33.

situations, which of course are susceptible to change. The absoluteness of God's commands would not be preserved but rather would be compromised if those commands were so general and vague that they applied equally to all situations.

Consider, for example, the sacrificial system. All believers recognize that the atoning work of Christ makes the Jewish sacrifices unnecessary. We agree that the various commands concerning animal sacrifices are not *applicable* today—that is, in the sense that they are not to be obeyed literally (although certainly they contain lessons that we can apply to our lives today). Does that fact suggest that the sacrificial laws did not have absolute divine authority? Of course they had such authority, unless we define *absolute* so as to preclude changes of any kind.

We may say that the situation (or context) created by the coming of Christ alters the way we, as part of this new situation, interpret the sacrificial system. We do not merely *apply* it differently, as would be argued by those who draw a sharp distinction between meaning (intended by the original author) and significance, or application. Rather, it would be accurate to say that we *interpret* that system differently; that is, we recognize now, in a way that could not have been recognized by the original audience, the essentially temporary character of those sacrifices.

In a very important sense, then, we contextualize the biblical passages in question without relativizing them in a way that undermines their authority. Quite the contrary, we thereby affirm that authority. If, on the other hand, we insisted that the sacrifices must be continued (as the recipients of the Epistle to the Hebrews appear to have argued), then we would indeed be violating the Word of God, which teaches us to look rather at the realities of which the Levitical system was but a shadow (Heb. 7:11–12; 9:8–12; 10:1).

This example, I admit, is rather simple, since the New Testament gives us explicit information regarding the temporary character of the sacrifices. Matters become a little more complicated when we consider the civil laws God imposed upon the nation of Israel; not surprisingly, Christians have failed to reach perfect agreement regarding their relevance. While we can find extreme positions on both sides of the issue, however, there seems to be a general (though ill-defined) consensus that the relevance of each of those laws should be considered individually.

In other words, rather than automatically dismissing or enforcing the Jewish civil laws, we should evaluate them within the framework of the teaching of Scripture as a whole. Generally speaking, then, believers recognize that some commands of Scripture, even if they are not explicitly superseded by subsequent biblical revelation, may have had a temporary or otherwise restricted significance. Conversely, we may feel obligated to act in certain ways not explicitly commanded in Scripture or to condemn certain modern practices not at all mentioned by the biblical writers on the grounds that our new context calls us to a fresh interpretation of the biblical message.

Unfortunately, these ideas are very easily subject to abuse, and some "progressive" Christians find in them a way to justify questionable practices, such as homosexuality. After all—so goes the argument—the church's view of slavery has changed dramatically in modern times. Is it not possible that other ethical standards may also represent so much cultural baggage?[15]

We need not overreact to this line of argument by rejecting the principles mentioned earlier. The proper response is rather to insist on the priority of grammatico-historical exegesis. It is here that the distinction between meaning and significance (though not to be absolutized itself) assumes crucial importance. We can hardly expect to contextualize a biblical passage in a responsible way unless we have first identified accurately its significance in the original context.

---

[15]Numerous works exploring the relevance of biblical ethics for our day have appeared in recent years. I have found none of them satisfying. A representative book that asks the tough questions within an evangelical framework is Richard Longenecker, *New Testament Social Ethics for Today* (Grand Rapids: Eerdmans, 1984). John Murray, *Principles of Conduct: Aspects of Biblical Ethics* (Grand Rapids: Eerdmans, 1957), appears too traditional to many contemporary readers, but they ignore this wise book to their peril.

It is worthwhile remembering that some practitioners of allegory in earlier centuries believed that allegorical interpretations should be tied in some way to the literal meaning of the text. How much more reason, then, for us who reject the allegorical method to make very sure that our attempts at reinterpreting the biblical text in the light of our modern context arise from a true appreciation of the original meaning. And this is just another way of saying that, in spite of contemporary claims to the contrary, emphasis on authorial intention must remain a major priority in biblical exegesis.

KANT AND BIBLICAL INTERPRETATION

We conclude, then, that our commitment to the divine authority of Scripture is not at all compromised by the recognition that shifting contexts often lead to a reinterpretation of the text. But what about the claim that our interpretive efforts themselves are engulfed by a cloud of subjectivity? In other words, even if we conclude that the Scriptures possess an enduring objective authority, is that objectivity perhaps unattainable by human beings?

In this case, the essential relativity of the *interpreter* supposedly prevents us from understanding the text. This particular objection is distinctively modern in character; in fact, it has been only during the past decade or two that the question has played a prominent role in biblical hermeneutics. (Even now the majority of biblical scholars basically ignore it in their actual exegetical work, though they may pay lip service to it in introductory comments and footnotes.)

Understandably, the history of interpretation gives us little direct help on this matter. Throughout the centuries it has been assumed without a second thought that our perception of data corresponds exactly with objective reality: if I see green grass, then it *must* really be green, and it must be grass! Now what is true of the scientific observer must surely be true as well of someone interpreting literature, though it might be recognized that in this case there is more room for ambiguity and misunderstanding.

Biblical interpreters in earlier centuries have of course been conscious of the role played by personal bias, but they have simply taken for granted that such a bias can be overcome. It certainly would not have occurred to them that in the very nature of the case we are incapable of grasping objective reality. Consequently, one searches in vain through their writings for interpretive methods or exegetical insights that might help us solve our contemporary dilemma.

On the other hand, it must not be thought that today's concern arose out of nowhere in the middle of the twentieth century. We can identify certain problems in the history of philosophy, even in the ancient period, that lie at its root. By common consent, however, it is with Immanuel Kant that we reach a watershed, a genuine turning point between modern thought and everything that preceded it. The effect of Kant's contribution was so broad and so fundamental in character that no intellectual discipline could escape its impact—not even biblical interpretation, though relatively few exegetes were conscious of what was happening.

We cannot describe Kantian philosophy within the confines of this little volume. We should remember, however, that Kant was deeply preoccupied with the unbearable tension that the Enlightenment had created between science and religion. (This issue was, of course, the old philosophical problem of reason versus faith, in new dress.) His own solution to the problem was to divorce the two.

Such a divorce involved a certain circumscribing of the roles performed by both. Religion, for example, must recognize its limitations: the basic tenets of faith cannot be proved by theoretical reason. But science is also restricted: observers never see things as they are in themselves, since the mind is no mere receptacle molded by physical sensations but rather is an active organ that brings order to the chaotic stream of data it confronts. In a very important sense, therefore, we may say that the world that is known to us is a world created by our own ordering of sensations.[16]

---

[16] In his *Critique of Pure Reason*, Kant had intended "to solve all the problems of metaphysics, and incidentally to save the absoluteness of science and the

To be sure, most scientists went about their work as though nothing had happened, but the seed had been sown for some fundamental changes in scientific outlook. Certainly, some of the most significant questions debated in twentieth-century philosophy of science concern the relativity of scientific thought. And if questions of this sort are being raised concerning a field that deals with highly "objective" experimentation, what are we to say about the more "subjective" tasks of literary interpretation? (Volume 3 in the present series explores some of these issues in more detail.)

What interests us for the moment is the effect of Kantian thought on nineteenth-century biblical interpretation. Kant himself, interestingly, reflected on this subject and suggested that we should approach the Bible in a way that sounds very much like a revival of allegorical interpretation.

> What may be required of the *art* of biblical *interpretation* . . . is . . . that the interpreter make clear to himself whether his statement should be understood as *authentic* or *doctrinal*. In the first case the interpretation must be literally (philologically) appropriate to the meaning of the author; in the second case, however, the writer has the freedom to write into the text (philosophically) that meaning which it has in exegesis, from a moral, practical point of view. . . . Therefore only the *doctrinal* interpretation, which does not need to know (empirically) what kind of meaning the holy author may have connected with his words, but rather what kind of doctrine the reason . . . can . . . read into the text of the Bible, only such a doctrinal interpreta-

---

essential truth of religion. What had the book really done? It had destroyed the naïve world of science, and limited it, if not in degree, certainly in scope, — and to a world confessedly of mere surface and appearance, beyond which it could issue only in farcical 'antinomies'; so science was 'saved'! The most eloquent and incisive portions of the book had argued that the objects of faith—a free and immortal soul, a benevolent creator—could never be proved by reason; so religion was 'saved'! No wonder the priests of Germany protested madly against this salvation, and revenged themselves by calling their dogs Immanuel Kant" (Will Durant, *The Story of Philosophy: The Lives and Opinions of the Greater Philosophers* [New York: Pocket Library, 1954; orig. 1926], pp. 274–75).

tion is the sole evangelical, biblical method of teaching the people in true, inner, and universal religion.[17]

Even more blatant is the conclusion reached by a notable liberal New Testament scholar, Hans Windisch:

> I claim for myself the privilege . . . of modernizing the assumedly historical Jesus for practical use, i.e. to work out a figure which is similar to the Jesus of Herrmann's theology. I am fully aware that I am reading subjective interpretations into what is historically provable and filling out gaps of scholarly research according to practical needs.[18]

FROM SCHLEIERMACHER TO BULTMANN

More systematic approaches to biblical hermeneutics on the basis of a post-Kantian world view were developed by several scholars. The so-called father of modern theology, Friedrich Schleiermacher, devoted considerable attention to this problem, and his writings are regarded as fundamental for the present discussion. Prior to his work, the discipline of biblical hermeneutics had not been carefully integrated into a general framework of human understanding. "An effective hermeneutics could only emerge in a mind which combined virtuosity of philological interpretation with genuine philosophic capacity. A man with such a mind was Schleiermacher."[19]

Of particular concern to us is his appreciation of the role played by the interpreter's presuppositions. Schleiermacher did not—as Windisch did many years later—use this principle to

---

[17]James M. Robinson's translation in his introduction to the reprint of Albert Schweitzer's *The Quest of the Historical Jesus* (New York: Macmillan, 1968), p. xvii.

[18]Ibid.

[19]From an influential article on "The Development of Hermeneutics," published in 1901 by W. Dilthey. The quotation is taken from *W. Dilthey: Selected Writings,* ed. and trans. H. P. Rickman (Cambridge: Cambridge University Press, 1976), p. 255. On the history of nineteenth- and twentieth-century hermeneutics, see esp. Stuhlmacher, *Vom Verstehen,* pp. 102–205, but note Richard B. Gaffin, Jr.'s caveats in his review, *WTJ* 43 (1980–81): 164–68. A more recent and very interesting analysis is that of Klaus Berger, *Exegese und Philosophie* (SBS 123/124; Stuttgart: Katholisches Bibelwerk, 1986).

justify arbitrary exegesis. He recognized, however, the significance of the "hermeneutical circle" and sought to incorporate it into a total hermeneutics.

> The understanding of a given statement is always based on something prior, of two sorts—a preliminary knowledge of human beings, a preliminary knowledge of the subject matter. . . .
> Complete knowledge always involves an apparent circle, that each part can be understood only out of the whole and to which it belongs, and vice versa. All knowledge which is scientific must be constructed in this way. . . . Thus it follows . . . that a text can never be understood right away.[20]

Toward the end of the nineteenth century, W. Dilthey, though interested primarily in the social sciences, made an important contribution to the analysis of human understanding and interpretation. Much of his own work was devoted to the role of the historian, a role that he believed required an actual experience of the past events being described. His notion of *Nacherleben*, which he viewed as the most important level of historical understanding, can be defined as

> a mode of re-experiencing which is to be understood as a re-creation (*Nachbildung*) of an expressed meaning rather than as a psychologistically conceived re-production (*Abbildung*). The

---

[20] F. D. E. Schleiermacher, *Hermeneutics: The Handwritten Manuscripts*, ed. H. Kimmerle, trans. J. Forstman (AARTT 1; Missoula, Mont.: Scholars Press, 1977), pp. 59 and 113; see also aphorisms 120–22 on pp. 59–60 and the discussion on pp. 115–16. Note the clear description by Rudolf A. Makkreel, *Dilthey: Philosopher of the Human Studies* (Princeton: Princeton University Press, 1975), pp. 264–66, on Schleiermacher's architectonic approach. For a somewhat tendentious treatment, see Palmer, *Hermeneutics*, pp. 84–97. Schleiermacher's application of his hermeneutical principle to theological construction was problematic, however: "Schleiermacher's contention that 'it is a most precarious procedure to quote Scripture passages in a dogmatic treatise and, besides, in itself quite inadequate' (*Glaubenslehre*, I, 30) was only a pretext to justify the unscriptural method of deriving the theological truths from his reason, or the 'pious self-consciousness' " (Theodore Mueller, *Christian Dogmatics: A Handbook of Doctrinal Theology for Pastors, Teachers, and Laymen* [St. Louis: Concordia, 1934], pp. 93–94).

creative understanding involved in *Nacherleben* is a function of the historian's imagination.[21]

From a somewhat different perspective, the British philosopher R. G. Collingwood took up this theme and emphasized the view that "the past is never a given fact which [the historian] can apprehend empirically by perception." Moreover, he "does not know the past by simply believing a witness"; in fact,

> he is aware that what he does to his so-called authorities is not to believe them but to criticize them. If then the historian has no direct or empirical knowledge of his facts, and no transmitted or testimoniary knowledge of them, what kind of knowledge has he: in other words, what must the historian do in order that he may know them?
>
> My historical review of the idea of history has resulted in the emergence of an answer to this question: namely, that *the historian must re-enact the past in his own mind.*[22]

Though Collingwood does not in this context appeal to Kant, the reader must perceive that these words could only have been written in a post-Kantian world. We need to reflect on the modern conception of historiography because biblical interpretation impinges repeatedly on the evaluation of historical narratives in Scripture. These related concerns come together in Rudolf Bultmann's coherent approach to hermeneutics.

As is well known, Bultmann had very little regard for the historical trustworthiness of biblical narrative, particularly the Gospels, and he appealed to the modern discussions regarding philosophy of history in support of his general approach.[23] Also

---

[21] Makkreel, *Dilthey*, p. 361. Makkreel, however, denies that "Dilthey supports a subjective, relativistic conception of philosophy" (pp. 6–7).

[22] R. G. Collingwood, *The Idea of History* (London: Oxford University Press, 1946), p. 282; my emphasis. He includes, incidentally, a perceptive analysis of Kant's view of history on pp. 93–104. On Collingwood's view of the historian's autonomy, see Royce G. Gruenler's comments in *HIB*, p. 580, building on the analysis of Cornelius Van Til.

[23] See Palmer, *Hermeneutics*, pp. 51–52. Bultmann's most important essays on this general subject have been brought together in *Bibel und Hermeneutik*, vol. 3 of *Gesammelte und nachgelassene Werke*, ed. H. Beintker et al. (Göttingen:

distinctive in his work is a great emphasis on the fact that we cannot do exegesis without presuppositions. In his view it is valid, and even inevitable, for a "modern" person to read the Bible from a naturalistic perspective, that is, with the assumption that God does not break into history. Since biblical narrative is full of supernatural motifs, modern interpreters are obliged to bring their preunderstanding to bear on the text, to strip the narrative from first-century myths, and to reclothe it with other myths (such as existentialist concepts) that make sense to modern culture.

While Bultmann himself did not take the next step of arguing that our subjectivity eliminates objective reality, we can see clearly how such a conclusion could and would be drawn by subsequent writers. We find, then, a fairly direct line from the Kantian dichotomy to the recent claim that biblical interpretation can have no objective significance at all. Part of our response must be to challenge the Kantian world view. The Bible itself knows nothing of a faith that requires some kind of compartmentalization so that scientific inquiry can proceed unhindered; nor does it allow us to think of reason as an entity that should leave religious commitment alone.

We also should note that no thinker seems willing to push the principle of subjectivity to its ultimate conclusion. Kant himself, for example, while he argued that we do not really know the nature of objects by themselves, added that "our mode of perceiving" those objects is shared by all human beings.[24] Brought in as if through a back door, Kant's

Vandenhoeck & Ruprecht, 1971); note esp. the 1956 article "Gotteswort und Menschenwort in der Bibel: Eine Untersuchung zu theologischer Grundfragen der Hermeneutik," pp. 138–89. His best-known article on hermeneutics was originally published in 1957 and translated as "Is Exegesis Without Presuppositions Possible?" This article is accessible in Rudolf Bultmann, *Existence and Faith: Shorter Writings of Rudolf Bultmann,* ed. Schubert M. Ogden (Cleveland: World, 1960), pp. 281–96.

[24] "We have intended, then, to say, that all our intuition is nothing but the representation of phenomena; that the things which we intuite, are not in themselves the same as our representations of them in intuition, nor are their relations in themselves so constituted as they appear to us; and that if we take away the subject, or even only the subjective constitution of our senses in

qualification salvages a very significant element of objectivity in scientific endeavor. Similarly, some of the most outspoken critics of objective interpretation themselves write with a marvelous assurance that their own words have a clear objective meaning that can be perceived by all their readers!

The solution to this problem is ultimately theological. John Calvin approached it brilliantly when he began his *Institutes* by raising the question of the knowledge of God. There are indeed many obstacles to our understanding of God and his message—our finitude, our corruption, and, yes, our relativity. But God himself is not circumscribed by any such limitation. He who created us knows how to speak to us. He who formed our minds knows how to reach them. The task of biblical interpretation is not an autonomous human endeavor but a response to God's command. And with God's command comes the power to fulfill that command. We therefore pray with Augustine, "Give what you command and command whatever you wish."[25]

---

general, then not only the nature and relations of objects in space and time, but even space and time themselves disappear; and that these, as phenomena, cannot exist in themselves, but only in us. What may be the nature of objects considered as things in themselves and without reference to the receptivity of our sensibility is quite unknown to us. We know nothing more than our own mode of perceiving them, which is peculiar to us, and which, though not of necessity pertaining to every animated being, is so to the whole human race" (Immanuel Kant, *Critique of Pure Reason,* trans. J. M. D. Meiklejohn, rev. ed. [New York: Colonian Press, 1898], p. 35).

[25] Augustine, *Confessions,* 10. 29 ("*Da quot iubes et iube quod vis*").

EPILOGUE

This book does not properly have a conclusion. We have sought only to identify and clarify the nature of the great hermeneutical task. Augustine's prayer, however, marks out the lines along which our solutions must be traced.

Consider the questions raised in the first chapter. The many disagreements that Christians discover in their reading of Scripture witness to the difficulties that face us in the work of biblical interpretation. We are now in a better position to appreciate what gives rise to different interpretations. A recent writer has argued that the real hermeneutical constraints "are provided by the interpreters" rather than the text and that "within very wide limits texts can be made compatible with interpretations." He adds, "Since it is a precondition of interpreting that what we interpret must be at least partially consistent and contain or indicate beliefs that we can share, we cannot . . . understand interpretations that challenge all our beliefs."[1]

The power of our hermeneutical predispositions makes growth a slow and often painful, *but not impossible,* process. Augustine's prayer teaches us that God is hardly a spectator from a distance, wondering how we will solve our problems. God is truly at work in the hearts of his people, causing us to grow together in unity unto the full measure of Christ (Eph. 4:11–16).

While the history of the Christian church contains many instances of discord, we cannot allow that fact to obscure the remarkable unity of understanding that has characterized God's

---

[1] Laurent Stern, "Hermeneutics and Intellectual History," *JHI* 46 (1985): 287–96, esp. pp. 293, 296.

people throughout the centuries. Precisely when one considers the numerous difficulties involved in reading an ancient document such as the Bible, touching as it does on many highly controversial issues, the great wonder is that the church has survived at all.

The history of biblical interpretation may be discouraging at times, but it also ought to reassure us that God has not left us alone. The evidence is plentiful that his Spirit has slowly guided believers to a fuller and increasingly clearer understanding of the divine revelation. And is not this progress sufficient grounds for assurance that he will continue to work in our hearts and minds as we devote ourselves to the study of his Word? The day will surely come when we will know fully, even as we are fully known (1 Cor. 13:12).

FOR FURTHER READING

A complete list of works cited may be found in the index of modern authors and titles. In this section I have selected contributions in English that should prove especially helpful as introductions to historical periods or to important figures. Most of them include bibliographical references to specialized articles and monographs.

Brief but substantive surveys of the history of interpretation may be found in the standard biblical encyclopedias. Note esp. K. Grobel, "Interpretation, History and Principles of," *IDB* 2:718–24, updated by several authors in the supplementary volume, pp. 436–56. Also useful is Daniel P. Fuller, "Interpretation, History of," *ISBE* 2:863–74. The most successful popularization is Robert M. Grant, *A Short History of the Interpretation of the Bible,* 2d ed. with additional material by David Tracy (Philadelphia: Fortress, 1984). Somewhat tendentious, but for that very reason instructive, is Peter Stuhlmacher, *Historical Criticism and Theological Interpretation of Scripture: Toward a Hermeneutics of Consent* (Philadelphia: Fortress, 1977).

Comprehensive histories of biblical interpretation are rare. There is nothing in English to replace the old work by Frederic W. Farrar, *History of Interpretation* (New York: E. P. Dutton, 1886), although Raymond E. Brown, *The Sensus Plenior of Scripture* (Baltimore: St. Mary's University, 1955), updates some important aspects. Fortunately, *The Cambridge History of the Bible,* ed. P. R. Ackroyd et al., 3 vols. (Cambridge: Cambridge University Press, 1963–70), while it does not provide a running narrative, covers all major areas clearly and competently. Histories of Christian theology usually touch on our subject; pride of place goes to Jaroslav Pelikan's magnificent achievement, *The Christian Tradition,* 5 vols. (Chicago: University of Chicago Press, 1971–). For a good selection of primary literature see James J. Megivern, *Official Catholic Teachings: Biblical Interpretation* (Wilmington, N.C.: McGrath, 1978).

Hermeneutics during the biblical period itself is treated most thoroughly by Michael A. Fishbane, *Biblical Interpretation in Ancient Israel* (Oxford: Clarendon, 1985), though his views on many specific texts are highly debatable. An excellent introduction may be found in part 1 of James L. Kugel and Rowan A. Greer, *Early Biblical Interpretation* (Library of Early Christianity [Philadelphia: Westminster, 1986]). The New Testament use of the Old Testament is a subject that would require a special bibliography; two useful surveys are the highly regarded conservative treatment by R. Longenecker, *Biblical Exegesis in the Apostolic Period* (Grand Rapids: Eerdmans, 1975), and a more recent work by A. T. Hanson, *The Living Utterances of God: The New Testament Exegesis of the Old* (London: Darton, Longman and Todd, 1983).

With reference to literature outside of the canonical Scriptures, note the following clear surveys: Samuel Sandmel, *Philo of Alexandria: An Introduction* (New York: Oxford University Press, 1979), esp. chap. 3; F. F. Bruce, *Biblical Exegesis in the Qumran Texts* (Grand Rapids: Eerdmans, 1959); G. W. E. Nickelsburg, *Jewish Literature between the Bible and the Mishnah: An Historical and Literary Introduction* (Philadelphia: Fortress, 1981), esp. chap. 7; and M. Mielziner, *Introduction to the Talmud,* 5th ed. (New York: Bloch, 1968), esp. pp. 117–87.

For studies of biblical interpretation in the ancient church we depend primarily on specialized works such as Alexander Kerrigan, *St. Cyril of Alexandria: Interpreter of the Old Testament* (AnBib 2 [Rome: Pontificio Istituto Biblico, 1952]), and Michael Andrew Fahey, *Cyprian and the Bible: A Study in Third-Century Exegesis* (BGBH 9 [Tübingen: J. C. B. Mohr, 1971]). More broadly conceived is the influential treatment by R. P. C. Hanson, *Allegory and Event: A Study of the Sources and Significance of Origen's Interpretation of Scripture* (London: SCM, 1959). Perhaps the best introduction to the methods of the Antiochene school is chap. 2 of D. S. Wallace-Hadrill, *Christian Antioch: A Study of Early Christian Thought in the East* (Cambridge: Cambridge University Press, 1982). Readings in the primary literature can be found in Karlfried Froehlich (trans. and ed.), *Biblical Interpretation in the Early Church* (Sources of Early Christian Thought [Philadelphia: Fortress, 1984]).

The medieval period has received good attention, especially in the work of Beryl Smalley, *The Study of the Bible in the Middle Ages,* 2d ed. (Oxford: Blackwell, 1952). Note also G. R. Evans, *The Language and Logic of the Bible,* 2 vols. (Cambridge: Cambridge University Press, 1984–86), as well as James Samuel Preus, *From Shadow to Promise: Old Testament Interpretation from Augustine to Young Luther* (Cambridge, Mass.: Belkamp, 1969). For a very helpful presentation of medieval Jewish hermeneutics, see Esra Shereshevsky, *Rashi: The Man and His World* (New York: Sepher-Hermon, 1982), esp. chap. 5.

Although we are lacking an adequate synthesis of Reformation hermeneutics, much can be gained from Ralph A. Bohlmann, *Principles of Biblical Interpretation in the Lutheran Confessions,* rev. ed. (St. Louis: Concordia, 1983). Otherwise, we depend on individual studies. A. Skevington Wood, *Luther's Principles of Biblical Interpretation* (London: Tyndale,

1960), is a brief but suggestive study. More detailed are Jaroslav Pelikan, *Luther the Expositor: Introduction to the Reformer's Exegetical Writings* (companion volume to *Luther's Works* [St. Louis: Concordia, 1959]), and Heinrich Bornkamm, *Luther and the Old Testament* (Philadelphia: Fortress, 1969). The best works on Calvin are T. H. L. Parker's two volumes: *Calvin's New Testament Commentaries* (Grand Rapids: Eerdmans, 1971) and *Calvin's Old Testament Commentaries* (Edinburgh: T. & T. Clark, 1986).

The development of modern critical methods is capably covered by W. G. Kümmel, *The New Testament: The History of the Investigation of Its Problems* (Nashville: Abingdon, 1972), which includes substantial excerpts from the scholars discussed in the text; S. Neill, *The Interpretation of the New Testament, 1861–1961* (London: Oxford University Press, 1964); and Emil G. Kraeling, *The Old Testament Since the Reformation* (London: Lutterworth, 1955). A briefer and more narrowly focused discussion is Edgar Krentz, *The Historical-Critical Method* (Guides to Biblical Scholarship [Philadelphia: Fortress, 1975]). For an in-depth and insightful treatment of one important subject, see Hans W. Frei, *The Eclipse of Biblical Narrative: A Study in Nineteenth Century Hermeneutics* (New Haven and London: Yale University Press, 1974). For the twentieth-century philosophical developments, see esp. Richard E. Palmer, *Hermeneutics: Interpretation Theory in Schleiermacher, Dilthey, Heidegger, and Gadamer* (Evanston: Northwestern University Press, 1969).

INDEX OF MODERN AUTHORS
AND TITLES

(Full bibliographical information may be found in the first reference to individual works. For a list of authors prior to the nineteenth century see the index of subjects.)

INDEX OF SUBJECTS

(All dates are A.D. unless otherwise noted.)

INDEX OF BIBLICAL PASSAGES